Francis Bennoch

Poems, Lyrics, Songs and Sonnets

Francis Bennoch

Poems, Lyrics, Songs and Sonnets

ISBN/EAN: 9783744777285

Printed in Europe, USA, Canada, Australia, Japan

Cover: Foto ©Thomas Meinert / pixelio.de

More available books at **www.hansebooks.com**

POEMS, LYRICS, SONGS,

AND SONNETS.

Poems, Lyrics, Songs,
and Sonnets.

BY

FRANCIS BENNOCH, F.S.A.

"Though no bold flight to thee belong,
And though thy lays, with conscious fear,
Shrink from judgment's eye severe,
Yet much I thank thee, Spirit of my Song,
For, lovely Muse! thy sweet employ
Exalts my soul, refines my breast,
Gives each pure pleasure keener zest,
And softens sorrow into pensive joy."
COLERIDGE.

LONDON:
HARDWICKE AND BOGUE,
192, PICCADILLY.
1877.

TO MY WIFE,

THE DEAR COMPANION OF MY MANHOOD,

AND EVER

MY TRUEST FRIEND AND BEST ADVISER,

I AFFECTIONATELY DEDICATE

THIS BOOK.

FRANCIS BENNOCH.

PREFACE.

NEARLY forty years ago I published a small volume of poems, which, to my surprise and delight, was most favourably received by the public. Reviewers spoke kindly of it; and several of the eminent poets of the time wrote to me encouragingly, whilst some advised me to adopt literature as a profession. But WORDSWORTH, in one of several letters, couched in friendliest language, whilst urging me to continue the study of poetry as a pleasure, quoted the opinion of

Sir WALTER SCOTT, that "poetry as a staff was a pleasant companion to walk with, but perilous as a crutch to lean upon;" and so I remained a man of business. At the same time I mingled freely and pleasantly with many of the foremost men in literature, art, and science. In some of the important movements in the metropolis, political, social, and charitable, it has been my good fortune to take an active part; and in connection with several of them my name is still united.

Like many others, I have enjoyed the blessings of prosperity, and like them too, suffered from adversity; but, whether lifted high by popular applause, or cast down by public forgetfulness, I have always found my sweetest consolation and dearest pleasure in my passion for poetry and in the practice of verse. My poems won for me the acquaintance and friendly correspondence of WORDSWORTH, SOUTHEY, LANDOR, KINGSLEY, DICKENS, HAYDON, Sir HENRY BISHOP, DE QUINCEY, CHARLES SWAIN, ALLAN CUNNINGHAM, —my Dalesman, whose kindness to me when a friendless youth in London, I ever gratefully remember,—and the fastidious ROGERS, who frequently received me as a welcome guest at his agreeable breakfast-table. They made me a companion of many of our present leaders in literature and art, whose names for obvious reasons need not be printed here. Through my verses I was introduced to the late MARY RUSSELL MITFORD. I was her visitor once a fortnight, for several years previous to her death. To me she committed the pleasure of gathering together and arranging for publication her Dramatic Works, and to me they were dedicated.

That a volume so unpretending as mine should have had so wide an influence has ever been to me a pleasant enigma. Yet, in addition to the names already referred to, it made me intimate with men of thought in France and Italy; but more especially in Germany, where FREILEGRATH (alas! no more), KINKEL, and CARL ELZE became my fast friends; whilst in America I was honoured with the esteem of BRYANT, LONGFELLOW, BAYARD TAYLOR, GRACE GREENWOOD, and that most genial of men, JAMES T. FIELDS. But, above all, it opened to me the heart of NATHANIEL HAWTHORNE, of whom I hardly dare venture to write. During the whole period of his residence in England we were as brothers. My house was as his own home, and to me more than to any living man, was disclosed the inner workings of his marvellous genius. Retiring, modest, and silent in general society; he was ever joyous, outspoken, and cheerful with me. Those who read his English Notes will discover how intimate we were, and will judge how sacred I have held the privilege of such a friendship.

At various times I have been urged to collect into a volume my scattered verses, but I have steadily declined to do so until I should be free from the daily anxiety of a mercantile life. Having slackened the cords and eased the collar of labour, I have now assented; and this volume is the result. Perhaps it is unwise, possibly foolish; for the world can well allow such verses to drift into oblivion, or remain in their present comparative obscurity. Yet, when I find many of my rhymes from time to time reappearing in the press, all over the world, and occasionally honoured by being chosen for selections of English poetry,—and sometimes with other names attached,—I think the time has come when I may fairly claim them as my own, and that this collection, may be looked upon as, at most, an act of pardonable vanity.

The compositions having extended over many years, a considerable diversity,—and possibly some incongruity,—of thought will doubtless appear. Condensation and not diffuseness has ever been my aim in writing. Having due regard to rhythm and harmonious cadence, my theory and practice has been to clothe my thought in the clearest language I could at the moment command.

The local colouring and general description of scenery,—especially in the Scottish poems,—I know to be accurate, because they are drawn from nature. Even the terrors of the Winter are described from personal experience. As the son of a Scottish farmer, it was my delight, if not my duty, to assist the shepherd and servants for a long winter's night in a terrible storm; the object being to keep the sheep on the windward side of the fold, lest, if left on the leeward side for shelter, they should be smothered in the drift and lost.

In gathering together my scattered verses, as far as I have been able, I have enjoyed considerable pleasure, and been moved by many conflicting emotions arising from the reawakening of long-slumbering experiences. Poems unread for thirty years or more, arouse many pleasant and some painful memories. Their appearance now will, I dare say, surprise many of my associates, who have hitherto only looked upon me as a merchant, or as a hard-headed financier, to whom the beauties of nature or the graces of poetry could have little fascination. Here, however, is the book, and here I close my preface, with the full assurance that friends and readers, whether they open the book from kindliness or from curiosity, will give it whatever credit, and do it all the justice, it deserves.

FRANCIS BENNOCH.

19, TAVISTOCK SQUARE,
    June 25th, 1877.

CONTENTS.

	Page
THE Storm	1
Sir Ralph de Rayne and Lilian Grey	25
To the Memory of Godwin	45
The Mourner's Hope	47
The Wreck	54
The Foundling	58
Words	61
My Books	64

LYRICS, SONGS, AND SONNETS:

Hast thou a Friend?	67
Who dares to Scorn?	69
May-day	71
Life	76
Mansfield	78
My Bonnie Wee Wifie	81
A Thought	82
Our Wedding Day	83
Together	85
Love and Beauty	86
Our Ship	87
Truth and Honour	89
The Lime-tree	91
Sing, Lady, Sing	93
London	94
First Verses in an Album	96
The Switzer's Song	97

LYRICS, ETC. (*continued*):— Page
Past and Present 100
Florence Nightingale 102
The Irish Gleaner 104
O Say not they are Past Relief . . 106
Eva 107
Minnie's Isle 109
Song—My Dear Minnie Mine . . 111
"The Bud is on the Bough" . . . 113
The Lily of the Valley 114
The Cheery Auld Maid 116
A Railway Rhyme 119
My Lady 121
Autumn Thoughts 122
Hors de Combat 125
Our Polly 127
My Love 129
Come, Come, Come! 130
Good Morrow 131
Mary Milligan 133
Come! Gentle Spirit of the Spring . 135
Spring 137
May 139
A Spring Song 141
Marian 142
A History 143
To the Hills Away 144
Song for the Season 146
Song—The Setting Sun . . . 147
Reflections 148
O, What are You Doing? . . . 150
What Is It? 151
My Own 153
Masonic Song 154
Love and Marriage, in Five Stanzas . 157
Love's Consolation 159
Dying 161
Minnie an' Me 163
Adam Brown and Jeanie Kennedy . 165
The Auld, Auld Story—Lasses Beware 168
Coila 172
To the Memory of Burns . . . 175

CONTENTS. xvii

LYRICS, ETC. (*continued*) :—
                                                              Page

Nith	176
The Bard's Return	178
Nith Revisited	180
Tynron Glen—The Shinnel	182
Song—Send the Brimming Glasses Round	184
The Bonnie Banks o' Dee	186
Courtship	188
The Flower of Keir	190
The Dominie	192
Natural Philosophy	195
The Tocher	197
The Scottish Gathering	198
I Dinna Ken what is the Matter Ava	200
Pride Maun Learn to Fa!	203
My Johnny	206
Song—O Jenny was Bonny	208
My Bairnie	210
Song—Oh Life it is Dreary	212
The Parting	213
Margaret	214
Willie	215
To Isabel	216
The Dying Daughter	217
The Shepherd's Plaidie	219
The Bonnie Bird	220
Song—O Stay wi' me now, Lassie	221
Kate	222
The Covenanters	224
Sandy's Coming	226
The Hizzies	228
My Ain Wife	231
Commemorative Song	233
What's Her Name?	234
Wae's My Life	235
Nannie Bell	236
Song—O Steek the Door	238
Song—Dinna Hinner Me	240
I Will Lippen Thee, Lassie	242
Isa	244
On Receiving a Bunch of Violets	246
Glen Valentine	247

CONTENTS.

LYRICS, ETC. (*continued*):—

	Page
To My Mother	249
In Memoriam	251
The Bruised Flower	253
Over the Hills	255
The Maid of Alton Vale	256
Mary	258
The Piping Shepherd Boy	259
A Poet's Wife	261
A Poet's Daughter	262
Never Despair	263
To Nathaniel Hawthorne	265
A Sketch from Memory	268
What Love is Like	269
Fair and Brief	271
An Appeal for Peace	272
Lines Written During Illness	273
Love's Potency	274
My Spirit Love	275
Exile's Song	276
Welcome is Night	278
The Tide will Turn	279
Three Meetings	281
Wallissellen	283
Duchess of Argyle and Her Son	285
Neil Gow's Oak	287
Watching and Waiting	289
To Mary—Maiden	290
To Mary—Wife	292
The Fisher-boy's Vision	293
My Lady Love	295
The Time to Marry	297
Home Love	299
To Whom we Bow	300
Pity Me!	301
Musings in May, 1875	303
Bessie has Come	305
The Trance	306
Garpel Glen—A Memory	309
The East	311
The Dignity of Labour	314
Polish Exile's Dream	317

CONTENTS.

LYRICS, ETC. (*continued*):—   Page
    She Came Among Us 319
    I Canna be Fashed 321
    The Maiden's Friend 323
    Wooing and Wedding 325
    I Will Try 327

SONNETS:—
    Howard 330
    Wordsworth 331
    Haydon 332
    Napoleonic—I. 333
    Napoleonic—II. 334
    Garibaldi—I. 335
    Garibaldi—II. 336
    Addressed to Major James Walter . 337
    Promises 338
    April—I. 339
    April—II. 340
    Ariel—I. 341
    Ariel—II. 342
    E. S. Dallas 343
    J. G., on her Wedding Day . . 344
    Frederick Latreille . . . 345
    Nymph and Goat 346
    Gipsies 347
    Mrs. Lough 348
    Sir John and Lady Key . . 349
    Memory of James Locke . . 350
    Blackheath 351
    Père La Chaise 352
    Companions in Travel . . 353
    Dauphiny Alps—Grand Chartreuse . 354

SACRED:—
    The Lord's Prayer 356
    Hymn on Founding a School or Church . 357
    A Morning Hymn 359
    For Higher Life 360
    Hymn among the Alps—I. . . 361
    Among the Alps—II. . . . 362

SACRED (*continued*):— Page
   At Lausanne 363
   Prayer 364
   The Daughter of Jairus 365
   Martyrdom 367
   The Wayside Cross 369

NOTES 372

GLOSSARY 393

INTRODUCTORY.

ATHERED and garnered; in this
    volume stored
  My vagrant verses, long left father-
    less,
  Are here avowed my offspring. I
    confess
Their claims are just:—Now are their rights re-
    stored:
Such praise or blame as readers may accord,
  Mine be the merit, mine the faultiness.
If in their wanderings, they have left behind
  One dear remembrance on some kindred heart,
Lifted one care from off one weary mind,
  Evoked one smile, or soothed one bitter smart:
  Deep gratitude is mine! Again we part
Dear children of my brain:—Oh may ye find
  Some souls receptive of the TRUTH ye bring:
  The false will fall as dross, or light as chaff
    take wing.

THE STORM:

A POEM,

IN THREE PARTS.

"We sail the sea of life,—a calm one finds,
And one a tempest,—and, the voyage o'er,
Death is the quiet haven of us all!"—WORDSWORTH.

> "The sounding cataract
> Haunted me like a passion: the tall rock,
> The mountain, and the deep and gloomy wood,
> Their colours and their forms, were then to me
> An appetite; a feeling and a love,
> That had no need of a remoter charm
> By thoughts supplied, nor any interest
> Unborrowed from the eye."
> — WORDSWORTH.

THE STORM.

Part I.

THE Spring had come with gentle
    showers;
  And herbs and plants and trees and
    flowers
    Sprang into life as south winds blew
Soft on their bursting buds, and dew
Moistened their lips, whilst one by one
They opened their leaves to the morning sun,
Inhaling with pleasure the genial glow
Of his golden beams,—for they seemed to know
That their beautiful bloom from his light must
    flow.
As his rays on their bosoms danced awhile,
You might hear them grow as you saw them smile:
The humblest flower with its crimson streak
Displayed in the blush of its velvet cheek,
How deeply it felt though it could not speak!

  At such a season—such a scene,—
    When Nature flung on every one
  Her sweetest smiles from wood and green,
    A mother thus addressed her son

In a western isle—as he lingering stood—
And silently gazed on the sleepless flood:
"Stay thee, O stay thee! my hair has grown
        grey,
    My limbs they are tottering, weary, and old,
    Their life's blood runs watery, slowly, and cold,
And who will protect me when thou art away?"

"Urge me not, mother,—it must be so,—
But give me thy blessing before I go!"
Her bony fingers pressed his brow
    And played amid his raven hair,
Her eyes to Heaven were upward turned,
    And thus arose her earnest prayer:—
"O Holy Virgin, to thy care
    And love maternal, I confide
Mine only son, and wheresoe'er
    He wanders, be his shield and guide!"
Convulsed with grief, her words were drowned
By streaming tears that bathed the ground,—
A dreary pause,—she kissed her son,
And then, in broken speech, went on:
"My first,—my last,—my only boy,—
My life,—my love,—my hope,—my joy!
My thoughts are with thee night and day,
And, as thou lov'st thy mother, pray
    That He may all thy actions bless
Who only is the orphan's stay,
    The 'Father of the fatherless!'"

"I thank thee, my mother!—thy blessing is dear
To my soul as the sun to the dawning year,—
As drops of rain to the parchèd tongue,
As kisses of love when the heart is young!

Ere Winter comes with icy chain
  And clanks his fetters o'er the ground,
Dear mother, I'll return again
  And make thy heart with gladness bound:
I'll charm the wrinkles from thy brow,
Thy cheeks shall furrow not as now,—
Where burning rolls the stream of woe
Shall trickling tears of rapture flow;
Thy years declining then shall seem
To glide in smoothness like the stream
Whose waves in music pass our door
And gently break upon the shore:
Farewell—farewell—come good or ill,
Thy blessing, dear mother, will cheer me still!"

His boat was riding on the wave,—
Another kiss she fondly gave,
And tenderly embraced her son,—
A deep—deep sigh—and he was gone!
Away he skimmed,—as light as air,
Across the sea,—she knew not where!

"And he has gone!" the widow cried,
"A mother's joy,—a mother's pride,
Although his father's course be run,
His spirit liveth in the son;
So like his sire in mind and frame,
I could believe they were the same!
Sure Nature by some mystic art
Hath changed the old man to the new,
Or given the young the old man's heart,
To show what she has power to do,
And Maurice' self and Maurice' son
May not be reckoned *two*, but *one*!

But, oh! this bosom keenly knows
The hopes—the fears—the joys—the throes
Of pain the child its mother cost
At birth, when he and she were lost
For aught that human eye could see,—
   But both survived, and, ah! since then
The comfort he has brought to me!—
   A comfort unalloyed with pain
Till now—when from this lonely beach
My aged eye can scarcely reach
The ship that now like vapour dies
Betwixt the ocean and the skies,—
'Tis gone! O Heaven, thy will be done,—
To bless the mother shield the son!"

Maternal love!—maternal love!—
   What rapture lies within thy name!
For men below and Powers above
   Commend thy passion's holy flame!
The balm of life,—a deathless power
That fades not in affliction's hour,
Through all distresses burning still
Undimmed—unquenched—unquenchable!
When poor exhausted nature sleeps,
   Or sickness haunts the infant bed,
With anxious eye the mother keeps
   Untiring watch upon its head!
The only joy her thoughts afford
Is hope that health may be restored:
But that denied, 'tis still her prayer
That Heaven at least its life may spare!

Nor was the mother's passion shown
Too much in favour of her own:

The rich,—the poor,—the young,—the old
Alike the worth of Maurice told;
For he had been the friend of all
At wake, or fair, or funeral,—
No matter where, no matter when,
Still Maurice was the chief of men!
The wisest would with him converse,
The bravest would his deeds rehearse;
Though proud and jealous of their fame,
All bowed to his superior claim:
Nor maids were wooed, nor hearts were won,
That he was not advised upon!
The music of the maiden's tongue
His fame and virtues sweetly sung
In an old-fashioned, artless rhyme,
Composed in manner of that time
When neither sense nor truth was drowned
In long confusing streams of sound.

Part II.

THE air was mild and smooth the sea,
　　The waves were heaving tranquilly;
　　No storm beset the Pirate's home
　　Or lashed the billows into foam,
　　But all was gentle, placid, mild,
And smiling like a dreaming child,
Or like fair fields of waving grass
As summer breezes o'er them pass.
The vessel, like an eagle free,
Flew o'er the tide in majesty,
A soul-expanding, cheerful sight,—
Yet Maurice' heart was lone as night,
For heavy thoughts had o'er him come,
Thoughts of his mother and his home:
For he had left his native shore,
Never, perhaps, to tread it more,
And as his eyes would homeward turn,
He felt his heart and temples burn,
Nor could he their excitement still,
Or bend pulsation to his will;
As tears dropped trickling o'er his cheek,
He blushed to think himself so weak,
But, consecrate to filial love,
Each drop that fell was blessed above!

The morn and noon passed slowly by,
The evening's mantle veiled the sky:
The sea, by day so smooth and bright,
Is far more lovely seen by night,
When o'er old Ocean's wrinkled brow
The night has hung her silver bow,
And stars in myriads ope their eyes
To guide the footsteps of the wise,
And in the deep reflected lie
Till ocean seems a second sky,
And ships, like winged aërial cars,
Are voyaging among the stars!
Though Maurice' eyes were fixed on these,
 His thoughts were hovering near the spot,
Enclosed by widely-branching trees,
 Where stood his mother's lonely cot.
O! deem not Maurice thought of sleep
Upon the bosom of the deep,
Or laid his weary limbs to rest
Before his father-land he blessed ;
And she, his life's first, latest care,
Was not forgotten in the prayer.
And now the soul-depressing cloud
Of gloomy thoughts that, like a shroud,
Bound up his heart, was rent in twain,
And Maurice felt himself again,—
Awake to Nature's glorious scene,
The mighty sea, the sky serene,
The air that through the rigging played,
A stream of gentle music made,
In concert joined the deep-mouthed sea
As bass unto the melody,
And as their voices rose and fell
Young Maurice tuned this fond farewell:

THE STORM.

"Farewell to thee, Erin,
  My own beloved isle,
Where Truth, Love, and Virtue
  In all seasons smile:
Where'er I may wander,
  The land I love best,
Is my own beloved Ireland,
  Bright Isle of the West!

"Thy valleys are fertile
  As valleys can be,
A garden of beauty
  Walled round by the sea:
Thou, fav'rite of Heaven,
  Art surely caressed
As the darling of Nature,
  Fair Isle of the West!

"The clouds that hang o'er thee
  Shall soon disappear,
And bright eyes shall welcome
  An advent so dear;
While brave sons defend thee,
  With true hearts possessed,
All lands will befriend thee,
  Sweet Isle of the West!

"When death shall draw near me,
  As sure he will come,
I'll smile at the summons
  That beckons me home,
If at last from my cares
  And my troubles I rest
In repose on thy bosom,
  Dear Isle of the West!"

Now Maurice laid his head to rest
  And closed his eyes, but, ah, how vain!
Though rocked on ocean's wavy breast,
  Sleep would not come to soothe his brain.
The shortest night is long and drear
When gentle sleep will not come near;—
Thus Maurice felt, and as the light,
  Clothed in the dawning's sober grey,
Came forth to chase away the night,
  And usher in another day.
He raised him from his sleepless bed
With heavy heart and aching head,
Which like a thought were charmed away,
For now the ship was in the bay!
His pulse beat quick,—an instant more
And Maurice stood on England's shore!
" And this is England! this the land,
  The birth-place of the mighty dead!
I see her heroes round me stand,
  As now her rocky shores I tread!
I feel their spirits in me burn,
  And lofty thoughts my bosom swell;
At every step, and every turn,
  My heart throbs quicker; who can tell
The high emotions that arise
As now I gaze on these bright skies
That smile upon this isle so free,
The fair Betrothed of Liberty!"

Short time had he in England been
Before his tone was changed, I ween;
For oftentimes would he compare
His mother-land with this so fair,
And, lonely wand'ring on his way,

He, murmuring to himself, would say,
"We live beneath as clear a sky,
Our towering mountains rise as high,
Our rivers flow as broad and clear
As those that smile around me here,
Our plains are all as fresh and green
As any plains in England seen.
Our men as brave,—our maidens too
Are not less lovely nor less true;
Yet one with wealth is running o'er,
The other's naked, starved, and poor
They're bound by every holy tie
Of sister love and sympathy,
Their interests are all the same,
   Their laws in truth alike should be,—
They both assume the British name.
   And both assist to keep it free:
But O!—accursed Jealousy,
   That breaks the dearest ties on earth,
My mother-land, has ruined thee!
   Till Justice governs and gives birth
   To equal laws, and fosters worth,
Thy children must remain the slaves
Of factious demagogues and knaves!
But when the ruling powers shall dare
To hold the beam of Justice fair,
And walk where Nature points the way,
And make *their* laws *her* laws obey,
They'll find our murmurs cease, and see
A smiling land,—a peasantry
Obedient,—quiet,—happy,—free!"

When Maurice to those cities came,
The source of England's power and fame,

The heart that through her system sends
    The circulating stream of life,
Transforming foreign foes to friends,
    And conquering ruthless war and strife.
(All-powerful Commerce, unto thee
The bravest spirits bend the knee!)
O'erwhelmed and wrapped in deep amaze
Too great for speech, he could but gaze
And think the more; and while he thought,
Reflection the conviction brought
That Ireland's poverty and woe
From sad misgovernment must flow,
The great, indubitable cause,—
Unequal rights and partial laws!

Though Maurice knew his country's wrongs,
Yet he could Nature's blessings feel,
And gladly listen to her songs
That through the heart in music steal
Whilst wandering by the dales of Dove
And Matlock's shady bowers of love,
Or o'er the hills that intervene
Where wimpling rills run bright between!
He climbed delighted up the steep,
And traced that mazy cavern deep
Where hidden gems in millions sleep
Till, wakened by the taper's light,
Shines out the brilliant stalactite,
And dazzling ore and gleaming spars;
As if "ten thousand thousand" stars
Had left the azure dome of night,
That by their concentrated light
They might create a magic cell
Where should some guardian genii dwell.—

Within the centre,—down—down—down,—
A gloomy chasm's pitchy frown
Confounds the all-bewildered sight,—
It seems the prison-home of night!
There subterranean torrents run
Unblessed by either wind or sun,
From out its bowels dark arise
Low fainting sounds like strangled sighs,
As if these dungeons dark confined
The ruined souls of human kind.

Thus wandered Maurice whilst the Spring
With all its buds and blossoming
Had come and gone, and at its death
With deeper bloom and richer breath
The Summer came with the Summer's joy.
As merry at heart as a laughing boy
When he runs and bounds and laughs and sings
Till the joyous tear in his bright eye springs:—
On came she bounding in sunshine and rain,
Dancing in music o'er mountain and plain;
Blithe was her life, led in greenwoods and bowers,
Sweet was the music she drew from the flowers,
As he hung them and swung them on bending trees,
Homes for the insects and food for the bees;
Their petals were nourished with sunlight and dew
Till her love was returned in the odours they threw;
She bathed all their lips on the fading of light,
And tenderly folded them up for the night.
Fond watch o'er their pillows untiring she kept,
And kisses gave all till they slumbered and slept.

But Summer was robbed of her garments so green
When sunny-browed Autumn arose on the scene;

Ripe was his ruddy face,—firm was his tread,
His mantle was purple and yellow and red
And brown,—and the locks on his lofty brow
In richness and beauty were seen to grow
Like the yellowing ears of the ripening corn
Waved by the breath of the joyous morn.
His locks in their glory were fair to see
As the sunny waves of a golden sea.
He stretched out his arms and shook his head
Till the luscious fruits of the year were spread:
And the juice of the apple, plum, peach, grape,
    and pear
Brought gladness to all,—mirth everywhere!

The last of his locks from his crown was shorn
By a maiden whose cheek wore the blush of the
    morn:
It seemed as she twined it around her brow
Like a sunset cloud on a mountain of snow:
Mirth was let loose, and away went the strain
Till the concave of heaven returned it again:
From a *whisper*, the echoes to *thunder* increased
To welcome the Queen of the Harvest feast!
Men's woven hands were her holy throne,
And, O! she was lovely to look upon;
A spirit lay laughing within her blue eye,
A spirit of love that made young men sigh
As they bore her home o'er the daisied green,
The beautiful, innocent, harvest queen!
No monarch on earth was more happy, I'm sure,
Her heart was so light and her thoughts so pure!
What would I not venture, where would I not
    roam,
To be present again at a harvest-home!

Then rustling leaves from the trees fell down,
And the wingèd seeds by his breath were blown
Over the seas, bearing verdure and smiles
To the rugged crests of the distant Isles.
As blossoms dropped down on their wintry bed,
Men passed them unheeded and thought them
   dead;
But do they then die? or only rest,
To arise again like a spirit that's blest?

As Autumn was dying, no more would he crave
Than that maidens might sing him to sleep in his
   grave.
His calm spirit flitted as setteth the sun.
Giving smiles to the last and life when gone!

By this had Maurice travelled o'er
Long dreary wastes of moss and moor,
And long left far behind the halls,
The stately parks,—the waterfalls,
Which art has made with nature vie
To soothe the heart and charm the eye,
Where Chatsworth's mighty wonders stand,
The pride—the glory of our land!
And now he treads a different soil
Enriched by never-ending toil,
Where dwell fair maids and matrons wise,
And men whose courage never dies,—
For fairer, braver there are none
Beneath the circle of the sun,
Like flinty rocks their hearts are true,—
Where Scotland piles her mountains blue,
And heaven spreads its dark blue sky
O'er valleys green and mountains high.

For stern morality and worth,
Give me the regions of the North,
Whose every vale and wildest glen
Is peopled by a race of men
Whose sires for Freedom firmly stood,
And won it with their dearest blood;
The mound below,—the cairn on high
Direct you where her martyrs lie.
What Scottish arms have nobly done,
May still by Irish hearts be won;
Our country, now despoiled and bare,
And deeply wronged, need not despair.
Her sons are patriots brave and true,
And, nerved by Justice, shall subdue
The haughty spirits who presume
To make their native land the tomb
Of Liberty—the scoff and scorn
Of every land—Yes! they were born
For brighter things, and yet shall show
What men by moral strength may do,
And by their own exertions save
A land of freemen from the grave.

Thus felt young Maurice while he stood
And gazed on Nith's romantic flood,
Whose banks are chronicles that tell
Where brave men fought and strong men fell;
And here THAT POET wrote and sung,
His muse the praise of every tongue;
Grave pilgrims to that silent strand
Have come from many a distant land,
Braving the wide tumultuous wave
To shed a tear on Burns's grave!

Part III.

THE evening sky looked calm and clear
When Maurice passed through Durrisdeer.
In hope the evening star might lead
Him safely on to Wanloch head;
From whence 'twas his intent to stray
O'er moorlands wild and mountains grey,
To see the foam and hear the din
That ever roars in Cora linn:
Then take the river as a guide
To lead him down the banks of Clyde,
By bosky glen or leafy shaw,
Until he reached the Broomielaw,
From whence he soon might find a sail
To bear him to his native vale —
Where sate his aged mother, lone
And weary, watching for her son.

But, ah! how vain the wish of man!
His fairest hope,—his dearest plan,—
When seemingly within his power,
Will vanish like that fated flower
Whose beauty charms the human eye,
But at a touch will fade and die!

So on that eve,—too bright indeed,—
Old shepherds weather-wise could read,
By some faint streaks that crossed the sky,
A storm—a dreadful storm was nigh.
And scarce had Maurice passed the mill,
And clomb the breath-suspending hill,
When through the glens on every side
The gusty wind moaned like a tide,
And clouds began to overcast
The sky—and then in bitter blast
The Spirit of Winter arose on the air
With shivering limbs all naked and bare.
Born in the depths of an Iceland cave,
Cradled and nursed on a stormy wave,
He slumbered a season and then came forth.
His steeds were the bitterest winds of the North;
A freezing cloud was his whirling car;
Darkness and Fear were his heralds of war;
His icicle teeth did rattle and shake
Like a hurtling stone on a frozen lake,
Or the clattering bones of a gibbeted form,
That is driven about by the merciless storm;
His long skinny arms he waved in the breeze,
And stripped of their verdure the plants and the
       trees.
Wherever he snorted, his withering breath
All delicate beings crumbled in death!
Loud, loud were the shouts of his boisterous
       mirth,
As he scattered dismay o'er the smiling earth;
The clouds were rent as the storm was driven;
He howled and laughed in the face of Heaven!
From the hills came volumes of drifted snow,
Choking the rivers and streams below,

Which gasped for breath, as they slowly ran,
With gurgling sounds like a dying man.

Such was the spirit men trembled to hear,
As he roared o'er the summits of Durrisdeer,
And swept through the glens of a thousand rills,
And thundered away o'er the Pentland Hills,
Then back o'er the Lowthers bellowed again,
As though a fierce earthquake were riving in twain
The stubbornest rocks:—no longer were seen
The green grassy mountains of bonny Dalveen:
A storm so terrific, so loud in its roar,
Nor Carron nor Enterkin witnessed before;
And with it seemed mingling shrieks of despair,—
Woe, woe if a stranger were desolate there!

In that dread hour when danger's near,
 And fate hangs balanced in the air
'Twixt life and death, and hope and fear,
 Or smiling joy or wan despair,
So closely poised, a single hair
 Thrown in the scale would turn the beam,—
'Tis then that coward custom flies,
 And sov'reign nature reigns supreme;
By one strong impulse all are moved.
 There is no vain distinction then
Of sect or creed—all, all, are loved,
 Accepted, as becometh men!
The proudest heart that ever beat,
 The proudest she that ever smiled,
When danger comes, are mild and meek,
 And humble as a nursling child;
Then sister unto brother clings,
 And woman flies to man's embrace;

Her arms around his neck she flings,
    And, looking upwards in his face,
Her timid eyes protection seek,
    And find it ere the tongue can speak.
E'en bitterest foes on such a night
Forget their enmity and spite.

A father was list'ning, a mother was weeping,
Her young ones in terror around her were creeping,
Hiding their heads in the folds of her dress,
Afraid to look out on the wilderness;
(The very dogs to the corners crept
And howled in tune as the tempest swept.)
At every burst, the tempest's roar
Came whistling through the crazy door,
They'd start, and check the rising breath
With faces pale as ashy death:
How steadfastly their eyes were fixed,
    As in that awful hour they stood,
And gazed upon the stubborn pile
    Of knotty, crackling, blazing wood!
The storm without might thousands kill,
They felt the fire was heartsome still,—
But hark! again that sound was heard,
    A low,—a deep and hollow moan,—
A wild, wild shriek!—a heavy sigh—
    A long-continued dying groan!
It might be true, and yet they thought
    It also might be fancy's dream,
At such an hour,—in such a storm
    What will not o'er our senses gleam?
If true, then aid could not be given,
    'Twere vainly waging war with Heaven!

    *   *   *   *   *

The morn had come,—the storm was o'er,—
The tearing winds were heard no more;
The sun was shining on the hill,
And dancing o'er the frozen rill,
Each tree appeared a chandelier
With pendent crystals bright and clear!
That hoary sage the hawthorn tree
Seemed robbed of his vitality,
But not of his gems, for there they were
Like jewels twined in a dead man's hair!

'Twas painful to the eye that viewed
The wreck that o'er some vales was strewed;
There many stores of corn and hay
Were driven by the winds away,
And many a tree, that yesterday,
With leaves and branches brown and grey,
Waved proudly on the mountain's brow,
Now helped to stem the tide below;
And some, whose roots more deeply sunk,
Showed nothing but the blasted trunk;
And many a cottage where had shone
The laughing eye, and where the tone
Of many voices often flowed
In song to cheer the loved abode,
The blast had driven to the earth,
Entombing all their joy and mirth!
Thatch, roof, and rafters all were gone,
The ruined walls were left alone!
Where once the peaceful bed was made,
The drifted snow in heaps was laid.
Where once the happy maiden slept,
Her parents, sisters, brothers crept;
Their quivering lips most truly told

That they were perishing with cold!
Cold—very cold.—indeed, they stood
Without a home, or fire, or food,
And vainly on their fingers breathed
To keep them warm,—the snow that wreathed
Around, made icy tear-drops start
And bound the blood within the heart.
In sooth, such havoc had been hurled,—
It seemed the ruin of a world!

Then shepherds leave their vales below,
And wander 'mid the mountain's snow,
To see how all their flocks have sped,
How many living left or dead;
And many a sheep that day was found,
All lifeless frozen to the ground,
Like grey stones on the mountain's side,
Or rocks made white by ocean's tide;
Some few found shelter in the wood,—
And many, death in Carron's flood.
Before they came by that deep linn
Where unseen rolls the Enterkin,
Beside that dreary mountain road,—
Far, far from living man's abode,—
A corpse was found,—a stiffened mass!
 Stretched on his bed of snowy bent,
His back to earth,—his latest sigh
 In vain to Heaven for guidance went.
Oh, who would think that lumbering frame
 Did once a sentient spirit own,
Or dream that cold and frozen brain
 Was once the soul's exalted throne!
The ravens croaked around his head,
 And flapped their wings with sheer delight,

To think such dainty fare was made
    For them in the storm of yesternight!
The carrion-crow with the raven fought;
    They sprung and perched, and round they flew,
So greedy to gorge on the tenderest part,
    The frozen tongue or the eyeballs blue!
As men drew near, they fiercer were,
And louder screamed in wild despair,
For they could not see what mortals meant
In stealing away the nourishment
Which Heaven to them in the storm had sent!

And who is he whom Winter's breath
Has wafted to the shores of Death?
Whose is that well-proportioned form,
The victim of the deadly storm?
Oh, ask it not!—my eyes grow dim,—
To think such fate should visit *him*
Whose mother's alone in a Western Isle,
    And morning and evening looks over the sea,
Praying, "Merciful Heaven! send me my son:
    Safely, O safely return him to me!"
Ah! little thinks she that her boy so good
Now sleeps in the winter solitude,
And never dreams she that her son so brave
Will moulder soon in a stranger's grave!

The body was borne to the top of the hill
Where the Wanloch arises, a whispering rill,—
And further still they carried the dead
To a sheltered part of the hills of lead,
Where a deep, deep grave by them was made,
In which was the wreck of the traveller laid,

To sleep for a season in solitude there
At rest from the world, and free from care!

* * * *

Now he returneth fast to clay,
Whose life inspired this simple lay,—
His fame the spirit of our song,—
We need not now the tale prolong,
For it would rend your hearts to name
The woes that o'er his mother came,
When first the tidings home were brought,
And how they in her senses wrought.
As you have seen some lofty tower,
The victim of the lightning's power,
One moment stand in beauty high,
The next in shapeless ruins lie,—
So, ere the truth was half revealed,
The stricken widow stared and reeled,
Screamed forth a wild, hysteric yell,
Then raised her arms, and deathlike fell!
Then godlike reason was o'erthrown,
And frenzy sat upon its throne;
And to her weak and troubled brain
Her senses ne'er returned again.
Then she for days—two, three, or more—
   Would seem like placid infancy:
And still her walk was by the shore,
   And still her gaze was on the sea;
She oft would mark a lofty stone,
And name it as her Maurice' throne.
She thought him now some mighty king,
   And o'er the sea could view him come.
Then crowns of weeds and shells she'd bring
   To wreathe his brow when he came home,

And round her neck she'd hang as beads
Bright shells or daisies strung on reeds;
For she in dreams herself had seen
Proclaimed her son's anointed queen!
Oft she would after strangers run
Inquiring of them for her son,
Then pointing upwards to the sky,
Would show the place he owned on high:
Then, tittering, quickly turn away
With foolish laugh or childish lay!

Now calm as night,—then, wild as war,
Her piercing shrieks were heard afar.
With clasped hands and streaming hair,
She looked the picture of despair;
Then, in a moment, meek in prayer,
And, freed from paroxysms wild,
The pillow fondled as her child.
For many months she wasting lay
   Upon her bed; and then the frame
Beneath its heavy load gave way,
   And faded like a sinking flame.—
But, ah! it is a painful tale,
Before it let us draw the veil.

SIR RALPH DE RAYNE AND LILIAN GREY.

So long as Alban's church shall stand,
To tell its story to the land,
This legend ne'er shall pass away,
Of Ralph de Rayne and Lilian Grey.
Legend.

TO

THE LORD HIGH PRESIDENT

AND OTHER MEMBERS

OF

THE NOVIOMAGIAN BROTHERHOOD,[1]

𝔗𝔥𝔦𝔰 𝔏𝔢𝔤𝔢𝔫𝔡 𝔦𝔰 𝔇𝔢𝔡𝔦𝔠𝔞𝔱𝔢𝔡

AS A REMEMBRANCE OF THEIR VISIT TO

ST. ALBANS,

JULY, 1869.

BY THEIR LAUREATE.

[1] See Note 1.

A LEGEND OF THE ABBEY CHURCH, ST. ALBANS.[1]

THE Summer sun shone brightly down,
And burnished MARTYR ALBAN'S town,[1]
As, 'wakening from its drowsy state,
It rose for the approaching fête.

The clamorous bells in joyance rang,
The harpers harped, the minstrels sang,
Triumphal arches stripped the trees,
Gay banners fluttered in the breeze,
As, thronging through the narrow street,
Came buoyant youths and maidens sweet,
And sprightly dames, and stolid squires,
And youngsters clad in gay attires;
For she, the fairest of the land,
Had pledged her troth, would give her hand
To one right worthy, loved by all,—
SIR RALPH DE RAYNE, of VINTRY HALL:

---

[1] See Notes 2 and 3.

And now had come the nuptial-day
Of brave Sir Ralph and Lilian Grey.[1]

Bands trooped from Gorhambury's towers,[1]
From old St. Michael's shady bowers,[1]
From Royal Windsor's princely halls,
And Hatfield's ivy-mantled walls:
From Sopwell's cloisters, dark and low,[1]
Came hooded nuns in movement slow,
So prim, precise, demure, and staid,
They bring the brighter picture shade.
Think not they come to bless or cheer:
No! firm in purpose, proud, austere,—
Resolved to excommunicate
The gentle bride as renegate;
For she had come beneath their ban,
In listening to the vows of man
Against their creed, which blazoned stood
To guide the dreary sisterhood:
"The pure in heart should rise above
All passion-throes of human love."
They seemed so gentle—void of art—
They almost won the maiden's heart;
And yet she could not help but feel
That something more than holy zeal—
Seclusion stern—a weary call!—
The God of life demands from all.

So wonder not the dismal train,
Emerging from the neighbouring plain,
Should seek the Abbey Church, and there[1]
Denounce the recreant sister fair.

---

[1] See Notes 4, 5, 6, and 7.

Oh, what to them love, joy, or health?
They knew she had unbounded wealth,
Which, from the ages far away,
Concentred now in LILIAN GREY.
The loss of one might peril both,
Which made the pious sisters wroth—
Wrath keenly felt and undisguised:
Revenge was sweet—revenge they prized.

The curse a wandering monk had framed
The ABBESS as her own proclaimed.
Severe and cold, o'er her white face
No smile e'er crept with rippling grace,
Which, welling up, reveals the good
In kindly-hearted womanhood.
The lip compressed, the pallid cheek,
And deep-set eye, fell purpose speak.
To firmly seize and cast aside
All hindrances to power and pride.

Apart the ABBESS musing stood,
Conflicting passions stirred her blood,
A hidden fire was seen to burn,
Some secret thought she seemed to spurn;
In slow, deliberate undertone
She spoke—'twas well she stood alone:
" What if the maid my might defies?
What if her lord my threats despise?
I've that within my secret power
Will make the boldest blanch and cower.
Even at the altar, whilst they stand
Husband and wife, clasped hand in hand,
My voice shall rise—so loud and clear
That heaven, and earth, and hell may hear.—

Anathema!—that withering cry—
Go, sleepless live—unpardoned, die!"

An orphan child, the maiden fair
Was left beneath the Anness' care,
To cherish, guide, and recreate,
In manner worthy her estate.
Though kept within the cloisters' gloom,
The early bud was now in bloom,
The cheek assumed a richer dye,
A deeper lustre filled the eye:
With knowledge and experience grew
Impulsive yearnings, sweet and new—
A wider range, a deeper sense
Of woman's power and consequence;
Her thoughts, matured, refined, profuse,
Were ne'er designed for hidden use.
The sisters sought her heart to gain—
"*Perhaps as* ANNESS *she might reign.*"
But ere her term novitiate closed,
SIR RALPH a different life proposed.
Unknown to abbess, nurse, or guard,
They met, where none kept watch or ward,
Beneath the shade of arching trees,
Whose leaves made music in the breeze.
A fitter place could not have been
For knight and maid to woo unseen.

How many a day from morn till eve
The dull routine her soul would grieve!
Or if relieved by menial toil,
Her spirit would from all recoil.
In contrast to her murky cell,
Where sickly odours dankly dwell,

Was that serene and lovely sight,
The starry sky and moon so bright:
Why, self-immured, there die and rot,
Forgetting all, by all forgot,
When she, like any bird, might be
Uncaged, a being blest and free?

How sweet to feel his circling arm,
His pleasant breath, come soft and warm,
Or, looking up, believe his eyes
Were starry guides to Paradise!
The tale was told—the truth revealed,
And loving lips the compact sealed.

Tradition still with rapture swells,
As on the rare event it dwells,
On each minutest circumstance,
Of steed, and banneret, and lance;
How, in their dazzling suits arrayed,
Shone those who joined the cavalcade,
And formed a bridal train so gay,
As body-guard to LILIAN GREY.

Two noble pages tripped beside,
To urge, restrain, or gently guide
Her prancing palfrey, creamy white,
With gorgeous trappings all bedight,
Perfect in form—with ambling tread,
And archèd neck, and comely head,
With whinnying voice and ears elate,
As proud to bear so fair a freight.
O'er breezy fields they gaily moved,
Through winding lanes the blossoms loved,

Adown the sloping west they came,
Passed fields with poppies all aflame,
Skirting the miller's lake-like dam,[1]
Where swans in pride of plumage swam,
And over buried VERULAM,—
Old HEATHEN VERULAM, whose stones[1]
Were filched to build the church, whence tones
Of prayer and praise continuous rise,
In lifting spirits to the skies!
As our weak frames of dusty clay
Must toil and fret their little day,
With hope, and fear, and joy, and strife,
Preparing for a loftier life!

The bride alighted at the gate,
Where smiling dames her coming wait,
With swelling hearts and kindly eyes,
To greet the blushing sacrifice.
They quickly form a bridal train,
And up the aisle march twain and twain:
The matrons first, and then the bride,
Then rosy bridesmaids, side by side,
Who at the altar steps divide,
And stem awhile the flowing tide.

Three score of virgins, draped in white,
Bear baskets piled with blossoms bright,
To strew with flowers and leaflets rare
The pathway of the wedded pair;
Approach with measured step—defile,
And line with light the bending aisle:

---

[1] See Notes 8, 9, 10, and 11.

Youths, smiling, watched the dainty feet
Keep time to music low and sweet.
So fair a sight had seldom been
In sacred fane or palace seen.

A mason carving high—alone—
The stately column's clustered stone,[1]
Suspended work, to watch below
The ceaseless current's ebb and flow;
The graceful forms—the glistening eyes—
The whisperings sweet—the fond replies,
By which the cherished hope's revealed,
And hearts with love are touched and sealed.
He, musing, gazed until they seem
The mirror'd phantoms in a dream.
Transfixed was he:—when all were gone
He sat immovable as stone;
But never more resumed his skill—
The column stands unfinished still!

The church was filled above—below,
With ladies bright, a lovely show
Of rounded forms and radiant eyes,
Which sculptors might as models prize,—
When through the eager, waiting crowd
A whisper ran: "Behold a cloud,
Foreboding ill, inveils the sun!—
The hour-glass sand has nearly run!—
The bride awaits!—the bride's forgot!—
The laggard knight deserves her not!"

Uncertain as the winds—they change;
Now all rejoice, since HUBERT STRANGE,

---
[1] See Notes 10 and 11.

From off the high embattled tower,
Descried the nearing cloud of stour:
"Within a mile their plumes appear—
Soon, soon the bridegroom will be here!"

If others murmured, RALPH DE RAYNE
Might well of our neglect complain:
To him and his, in sooth, 'tis time
We bend the current of our rhyme.

From ancient hall and bustling town,
From grassy vale and upland brown,
The noblest, bravest of the land,
To swell the bridegroom's joyous band
Came coursing up with dawning light,
To cheer the heart, and please the sight,
So full of frolic, youth, and glee,
The flower of England's Chivalry.

A score of miles, or more, divide
The happy bridegroom from his bride;
And thus from VINTRY's fair abode
The gathered gallants early rode;
They rode through forests deep and dark,
O'er furzy heaths, by grange and park,
Through narrow ways—o'er open plains,
With gorges ploughed by recent rains.
On, on they rode with songs of mirth,
Whilst Summer sunshine bathed the earth.
Though most were handsome, fair and tall,
SIR RALPH rode high—a head o'er all;
In hawking, hunting, joust, or ring,
They were his subjects, he their king.

And when they reached the rounded height,
Whence ALBAN'S CHURCH appeared in sight,[1]
With reverence bowed each faithful knight.
The lovely view that met their eyes,
Awakened wonder and surprise:
The undulating valley green,
The sombre woods, the glades serene,
The glittering VER, in windings bright,
Like thread of molten silver white,—
What more on earth could man of bliss
Desire, than such a home as this?

A while entranced, they glad surveyed
The lovely scene of light and shade,
And half reluctant moved again,
Descending slowly to the plain.

Where two roads joined,—a dusky shade
By overhanging branches made,—
A moment's halt was called for, there
To set the train in order fair.

The word was given, again they move
Some paces on, beyond the grove,
Where stands the sculptured DRUID STONE.
Whence—why that shriek and heavy groan?
An arrow, shot from bow unseen,
Athwart the host, with glittering sheen,
Flew like a flickering bolt of light.
With point of steel and feather white,
And pierced the neck of RALPH DE RAYNE,[1]
Who prostrate fell upon the plain.

---

[1] See Notes 2 and 12, and "Bridal Song."

A quivering throb—a pool of gore—
In death he lay, to rise no more.

Alarmed, each knight his comrade scanned,
Each fearing each the deed had planned.
Whilst all, with consternation blind,
Stood still, the traitor slipped behind,
And quickly sprang the bank, and flew
For refuge in the Forest New.
It happed, that whilst he urged his horse
Through tangled ways of fern and gorse,
A knight who'd wandered from the throng,
A minstrel knight, who conned a song,—
A bridal song, of smiles and sighs,[1]
To win applause from ladies' eyes—
Brave MONTE ROCCO, from PROVENCE,
Who deftly plied sword, pen, and lance,
Was roused from his delicious dream,
When flashed across his eyes a gleam,
Reflected clear from polished steel.
He started—paused—with lifted heel
Stood high—beheld a cowering knight
Retreating from the troop in flight.
Suspecting cowardice, or wrong,
He thought no more of tune or song;
Nor reasoned he—the impulse given
Seemed inspiration straight from heaven.
He clutched the rein—clipped close the knee,
For none his Arab steed could flee.
Resolved at once, he gave him chase—
'Twas pity few beheld the race!
With every bound of flying BESS,

---

[1] See "Bridal Song."

The space between grew less and less,
As nearer and more near he drew,
Too well the crouching knight he knew.
Swift as the lightning's scathing flash,
His glittering blade was drawn, and crash
Through casque of steel, of azure hue,
He clove the grizzly head in two:
As down the unerring falchion fell,
Up rose, released, a hideous yell,
In circles, eddying round and round,
Till swallowed by the yawning ground;
The gibing laugh, the dying wail,
Made even MONTE ROCCO quail.
Recovering from his sense of dread,
He thus apostrophised the dead:
"Oh! Heaven is just, and will avenge;
I now my sister's wrongs revenge!
'Tis thou, false ULRIC! false as hell,
Near whom no innocence could dwell;
A recreant knight—a Monk foresworn,
To rapine, lust, and murder born;
Abjured of Heaven, thou hast thy doom,
And hell might well deny thee room!
I thank the POWER SUPREME, DIVINE,
Thy work, accursed, is stayed by mine!"

The spirit freed would homeward go,
The carcass fed the wolf and crow;
The avenging knight recrossed the plain,
To join the weeping wedding train;
A truer knight ne'er poised a lance,
Than MONTE ROCCO, of PROVENCE.

Whilst noble hearts for vengeance burn,
Now to the Abbey Church we turn,

Where all in expectation wait:
The Priest in grand array of state,[1]
With crozier, crucifix, and hood,
Near the exalted altar stood,
To give his benedictive sign,
And make the civil bond Divine.

Why shrinks the bride? why turns she pale?
Why clings she to the altar rail?
With eyes fixed on the iron grate,
Where great Duke Humphrey lies in state,[2]
Before her glistering, glaring eyes,
A shadowy form is seen to rise;
'Neath raiment, thin as woven dew,
A spectre form is beaming through,
With lifted hand and sunny smile,
Comes noiseless up the stony aisle.
Unchecked, through all, she sees it glide—
Now—now 'tis standing by her side;
And oozing down from neck to chest,
A trickling crimson stains the vest!
She nothing feels, and yet can see
The form droop slowly to its knee;
Her hand it gently raised, and pressed
With tender fondness to its breast,
And on her finger placed a ring.
Whilst faint seraphic voices sing
A strain that told of love and home,
The sweet refrain—"*Beloved, come!*"
Enrapt, she listened to the theme,
That seemed like music in a dream.
Another form she then beheld,

---

[1] See Note 13.   [2] See Note 14.

A form well known in days of eld,
With areoled brow—one hand outspread,
Which wreath-like rays effulgent shed,
That seemed to rest on either head.
His left hand held a feathery palm,[1]
His face out-beamed with heavenly calm.
'Twas HOLY ALBAN, from his throne
Come down, to bless them as his own,
And, blessing, faded from her sight
As clouds are melted into light.
In vain she strove to move or speak,
And aid from her betrothed would seek.
All dumb and motionless she stood,
Till glancing on the HOLY ROOD[1]
She turned—would speak to RALPH—but where
She thought he stood was empty air!
With claspèd hands she stared with awe,
As she alone the vision saw.

The matrons start, with looks amazed,
Cry "Hartshorn! ho! the bride is crazed!"
As quick to help they all approach,
And on the altar steps encroach ;
When, with a calm beseeching eye,
An upturned look, a stifled sigh,
She raised her hand and whispered "Stay!"
Then bent as if she meant to pray.
A silence spread profound o'er all,
You might have heard a feather fall.
When, through the yielding air, so still,
Was heard a sweet faint voice, "I will!"
As died away the thrilling sound,
Fair LILIAN fainted to the ground.

[1] See Notes 15, 16, and 17.

Aghast, spectators held their breath,
"Can this be feigned, or is it death?"
They first recoiled, then forward crushed,
But in a moment all were hushed.
The mitred priest stooped down to see,
And raised the lady to his knee;
Her lily temples gently pressed,
And placed his palm upon her breast:—
"Alas, alas! her days are o'er,
Fair LILIAN sleeps to wake no more!"

The joyous sounds that rode the gale,
Had now become a funeral wail;
The cheeks that swelled with lusty cheers,
Were channelled now by streaming tears;
As through the thinly peopled vale
Spread wide the strange and piteous tale;
Too soon 'twas known, SIR RALPH DE RAYNE
Had all unshrived been foully slain.
The instant brave SIR RALPH had died,
That moment sank his lovely bride;
Though lost, yet found—to them 'twas given,
To wing as one their flight to heaven.

The minstrel's song was left unsung,
The curses wild were left unflung;
The blossoms rare were left unstrewed,
Like statues there the maidens stood;
One heavy, all-absorbing grief
Oppressed them, till they found relief
In sighs and sobs, and scalding tears,
Which o'er their cheeks in glistening spheres
Rolled rapidly, and as they rolled,
Of sympathising anguish told.

Soon, soon within the transept's shade
A bier was raised—the bodies laid;
Bells ring with muffled murmurs low,
The incense rises, candles glow;
From fretted roof and cloisters dim [1]
Resounds the solemn requiem.[2]
How beautiful!—there, side by side,
His left arm pillowing his bride;
Not clothed in robes of sable night,
But in their wedding raiment bright!
Death may divide—death here has wed,
The bier become their bridal bed!
No clouds by night shut out the stars,
No mist by day the sunshine mars;
The cloudless sky, serene and deep,
Seems watching o'er them as they sleep.

With Sabbath dawning spread a cloud
Enshrouding all the sky; a crowd
Of silent mourners came—each brow
With cypress wreath was circled now.
Within the chancel's solemn gloom
Was made a deep, a holy tomb:
Where gently were together laid
The brave young knight and lovely maid.
The entrance bore this legend—Pray
For Ralph de Rayne and Lilian Grey.

But ere their radiant forms were hid
From loving eyes by coffin lid,
The bridesmaids came, and, pleading sought

---

[1] See Note 18.   [2] See "Requiem."

The veil and wreath their hands had wrought,[1]
Should in the church suspended be,
That every coming age might see,
In those memorials fair, but frail,
The germs of this our touching tale.

And there the relics hang on high,
And Time's destroying touch defy:
For year by year young virgins strew
The church with flowers, the wreath renew.
So long as ALBAN'S CHURCH shall stand,
To tell its story to the land,
This legend ne'er shall pass away,
Of RALPH DE RAYNE AND LILIAN GREY.

BRIDAL SONG.

BY MONTE ROCCO.

MERRILY, merrily, ring the bells—
    Ring the bells—ring the bells!
    O'er hill and plain, the sweet refrain,
    In sounding joy, melodious swells.
Ring the bells, ring the bells;
Oh, merrily ring the bridal bells!

---

[1] See Notes 19 and 20.

They come, they come, the vale along,
 Like morning beams the gentle bride;
They come, they come, with lyre and song,
 The bridegroom moves with manly pride.
  Ring the bells, ring the bells;
  Oh, merrily ring the bridal bells!

Now—now the pealing organ sounds
 In cadence low, or loud and clear,
Till every heart with rapture bounds:
 Oh! blessings are rained in music here.
  The organ swells, the organ swells,[1]
  How grandly now the organ swells!

Again, oh! merrily ring the bells,
 Ring the bells, ring the bells!
The rite is done, the two are one,
 Each heart with joy unbounded swells.
  Ring the bells, ring the bells;
  Oh, merrily ring the marriage bells!

REQUIEM.

DOWN, adown, adown, in the deep dark tomb are laid
Our brave young knight, our lady bright, the grave their bridal bed.
 The sun that rose so full of joy has set in misty clouds:

---

[1] See Note 21.

The bride who should a wife have been, the veil
  of death enshrouds,
And by her side the bridegroom lies—all still his
  manly voice.
There let them rest, for they are blest, and we
  may well rejoice,
  That brave young knight and lady bright should
    peacefully be laid
    Adown, adown; adown, adown,—shower
      blossoms on their bed.

Above, above, above, beyond the blue serene,
Our brave young knight, our lady bright, are
  with the angels seen;
Their robes of clay are cast away, and far beyond
  the clouds
They wing their flight to realms of light which
  sorrow never shrouds:
On! side by side, beyond the tide, which life from
  death divides,
As one they sing with seraphim where endless
  love abides.
The spirits bright of maid and knight from
  trouble are at rest,
Above, above; above, above, in regions of the
  blest.

TO THE MEMORY OF GODWIN.

WRITTEN ON THE ANNIVERSARY OF HIS BIRTHDAY.

DEAD! is he dead? stern advocate of truth,
   Godwin the just, the generous, the good?
   No! Godwin lives, and every man and youth,
Whose soul with love for liberty's imbued,
Will ever honour him with reverent gratitude.

His mind was like a meteor in the sky,
   Beaming in brightness through the hazy gloom
Of error—showing chained humanity
   Its noblest path to freedom, and its doom.
   To Truth he raised a fane on Custom's mouldering tomb.

When kings and priests, and parasites, as wind
   Have passed into oblivion dark and drear,
Godwin shall reign in every thinking mind.
   Whilst truth and wisdom unto man are dear,
   His name from many eyes shall draw joy's trickling tear.

To him shall unborn nations look with joy;—
  His noble works are like a mighty stream,
Sweeping before them vices that alloy,
  Till glowing hearts with spring-like freshness teem.
  Where once corruption grew, shall fruitful knowledge beam.

Hail to the morn that gave the patriot birth,
  Hail to His genius—it shall perish never;
Whilst time and tide roll on, or moves the earth,
  Godwin from men's best feelings nought can sever;
  His soul is in his works, and they shall live for ever!

THE MOURNER'S HOPE.

WHEN sultry noon has faded into
  eve,
  And cooling breezes round my
    temples play,
  Wafting sweet odours from the
woods and hills,
I love to wander with my gentle boy;
First-born of her who was my youth's delight,
My manhood's stay, and now is memory's pride.
How beautiful she was!—how loved by all!—
Her thoughts how noble, and her deeds how pure!
Her spirit all too eager for its frame,
So lovely, yet so frail,—the heart's delight,
And yet its fear;—she lived like some sweet plant,
That bends its head beneath the noiseless breath
Of Summer's eve, and ever as it bends
Throws off a part of life that never dies,
But gives new joy to others,—feeding all
That come within the circle of its power:
Each pearly drop of odour-spreading dew
That falls from out its honied lips, gives drink
And gladness to the thirsty earth, for thus
In tenderest love reciprocal they feed
Each other,—mutual in exchange of gifts,

And richer by exchange. Such was the wife
I loved,—all hearts in reverence blessed her name
Whose bounty was of Heaven, and so bestowed
That poor recipients could not help but feel
They almost granted favour to receive!

Thus was her kindness dealt,—no outward show
Of pomp or self-exalting vanity
That turns the starving beggar from the door,
And ne'er confers a charity on man,
Unless the action be with due parade
Emblazoned forth upon the wingèd sheet
That flies around the habitable globe;
But wheresoe'er was darkness and distress,
Her searching eye brought light and lasting joy!

Alas! her day of usefulness is o'er;
In one unguarded moment, while she strove
To ease the sufferings of a fainting heart
That lay neglected in a wretched cell,
Forgetful of herself and where she stood,
That wily thief, CONSUMPTION, marked his prey.
And, with the damp and noisome atmosphere
She breathed, he crept into her heart, and spread
His poisonous vapours through her azure veins,
And, like a friend deceitful, smiling sat
Plucking the roses from her comely cheeks,
Till Death, with all his melancholy train,
Swept o'er her heart and bore her life away!
She slept,—she died,—how cold, how beautiful!
The smile upon her marbling cheek was stayed,
And made her to imagination seem
The sculptured form of happiness asleep:
Like plaintive strains of music borne away

Upon the balmy gale of night, that glide
So softly into silence, none can tell
Where music ends and silence first begins,
Her spirit passed away to realms on high.

One gloomy coffin, and one narrow grave,
In darkness hide the form of her I loved;
And, cradled on her bosom in sweet sleep,
Two unblown buds of immortality!
Breathe softly o'er their tomb, ye winter winds;
And O, ye summer showers, fall gently down
And mingle with the consecrated earth,
That kindly feeds the rose-tree planted there,
Whose fragrance, like her soul, can never die!

O woe is me to mourn my hapless fate!
O why has Heaven this heavy burden laid!
What wicked crime doth load this dreary heart,
That thus should come so great a punishment?
Alas! I made an idol of my love,
And Heaven, whose rod is mercy, broke the charm,
And bore *her* hence, to teach *me* how to live!
Through all this depth of melancholy gloom
I see bright rays of never-dying Hope
Diverging from my boy,—my noble boy,—
For whom my soul's solicitude in prayer
To Heaven ascends at morning when I rise,
And ere at night I sleep.—O, not in vain!—
His little voice is music to my ears,
Whene'er with solemn feelings he repeats
The hymn of eve or morn, or prayer of Christ,
His mother's lessons in her dying hour!
How beautiful is piety in all!
But O! most beautiful in tender youth,

Where age may see the image of itself,
Stripped of the bare decrepitude of years,
Look out in spirit from the beaming eye
That speaks "Immortal is the human soul!"

I would not cramp his tender mind with books,
But spread before him Nature's glowing page,
In hope to teach high principles of Love.
In all things tracing the result of plan,
Of knowledge infinite,—of wisdom vast;—
Beginning with the objects clear to sense,
Then rising to the world beyond our view,
To treat of things invisible,—sublime,—
Of Him, the all-in-all creative mind,
The glorious centre of a wondrous whole:
Thus in the mind would I foundation lay,
To raise a temple consecrate to God,
A being worthy of the name of Man!

It was but yester-eve my gentle boy
And I, as is our wont, went rambling on
Through many scenes that Time has rendered dear.
Young Memory was alive, had spread her wings,
Had borne me over mountain, moor, and plain,
And placed me wandering in my native vale,
Far, far away,—the home of peace and joy!
And O! such pictures of the past she drew,
As realizes heaven to man on earth!
The sun was sinking in the glowing west,
The yellow clouds were floating on the air
Like ships of gold upon an azure sea,
Freighted with spirits blest, sailing to heaven.
The breeze was charged with melody, sweet sounds
From birds, and humming bees returning home,

Laden with sweetest treasure from the hills
To cheer the young things in their lonely cells,
And food in plenty ; store against the time
When winds blow chill and hills are bleak and bare:
A lesson most significant to man !
Anon, the shepherd's pipe, the lowing kine,
The gentle lambkins bleating in the fold.
The whistling of the lazy hind, from toil
Returning with his team, the milkmaid's song.
The choir of minstrels on their leafy boughs,
The city's hum, the babbling stream, the chime
Of evening mingling made a concert wild,
Most natural—most beautiful and dear !

Soon, one by one, these voices all were hushed ;
Star after star with twinkling eye arose ;
The new-born moon came climbing up the dome
Of heaven's ethereal vault ; her languid smiles,
Though winsome, were as coldly drear as those
Dim lights which superstitious legends hang
With purple flame around the sepulchre ;
And still I love the quiet twilight moon—
She cools the fever of my busy brain.
And in her ceaseless wanderings with one
Devoted star attendant, seems to me
The prototype of self.

All nature now was silent in repose ;
The present seemed the stillness of the grave,
And sleeping flowers flung out their odorous
       breath,
Filling the air and every sense with balm.
In silent contemplation still I walked
Unfit companion for a lively boy,

Whose questions rapid as a torrent flowed,
Untired, untiring. Looking in my face,
He marked the changes thought had written there,
Then dropped my hand and, stooping to the ground,
Picked up a stone and flung it in the air,
Which in its course made music: "Look," he cried,
"That senseless stone has more of life and life's
Companionship than has my father now."
I felt the child's rebuke steal through my heart,
And fill its deep recesses with regret.
Anon he danced, he leaped, he laughed, and made
My youth return,—I felt, like him, a boy!
And now his eyes were fixed upon a star,
Bright Venus, rising in her loveliness.
Gazing intently for a while, he cried,
"O that the heavens were indeed my home!
Their walls so wide, their roof so blue and high,
The windows all so beautifully bright;
The sun, the moon, the stars, and that great star
So brilliant in itself, is like—" "Like what?"
" The diamond glittering on my father's breast;
But larger, brighter; every star's a world,
A world where angels dwell: if so, O then
That star may be my mother's heavenly home,
And from that home she watches what we do,—
O father, how I wish that I were there!
What joy to see again my mother's face,
To feel again her hand smooth down my hair,
To feel again her kisses till I slept!"

Wondering, I gazed upon my own dear boy,
And clasped him to my beating heart,—my child,—
How dearly then I loved my darling child!
I brushed the hair from off his radiant brow,

So high, so wide, and kissed him with delight,
And looking through his beaming eye, beheld
His mother's soul revealed; those eyes her own,
So full of hope, of piety, of love!
I felt her sainted spirit in me burn,
I blessed the mother while I blessed the child,
And, blessing, kissed him o'er and o'er, until
My heart gave way, and like a child I wept!

1838.

THE REBUKE.

H be not rash, condemning all!
   Condemn not *one*, not one despise;
   Whate'er his crime, whate'er his fall,
However deep, he yet may rise
Through timely aid, for aid brings peace,
   And *that* repentance: thus is given
To man, by God, a power on earth,
   To win an erring soul to heaven!

THE WRECK.

FRAGMENTARY SKETCH AT HASTINGS.

I CLIMBED up the cliff and the castle high,
And wistfully gazed upon sea and sky;
The limitless sea, in its great unrest,
Made yeasty the waves on its billowy breast;
They would clasp at the moon in their eager love
To learn the passion by which they move.
They rolled and fretted with silver the strand,
Lapping the shingly, serrated sand,
As a spaniel will lick its protector's hand.

Far, far away in the crimsoned west,
The great sun sank to his pillowy rest,
Lay down like a king on his ocean bed,
With a gilded crown on his Royal head.
Embroidered with silver and gold and blue,
And gay were the curtain clouds; and through
The chasms, a distant depth was seen
All dazzling opal, blue, and green,
Whilst tufts of clouds bedappled the sky,

Befringed with a lustrous blood-red dye,
The broad sails under shone ghastly white
When smitten with fitful flashes of light;
They passed and crossed all over the sea;
Like shuttles of doom, they seemed to me
To be weaving a web eternally.
A web of commerce for all the world;
The fast waves following, dashed and curled
Their feathery lips, as the cleaving prow
Spread ever a widening wake of snow.
Far off in the west the sky was marred
By level clouds rifted, gashed, and scarred,
By a rising wind which cut like a sword,
Making way for the lightning's awful word.

The gold had faded, the sky looked pale,
And methought I heard in the rising gale
A long, long scream, then a dying wail,
From beyond the cliffs, whose white teeth rise,
Like the teeth of a tiger when crouched he lies,
Awaiting his victim with flashing eyes.
He springs—the traveller shrieks and dies.

Again came the wail, now near, then afar,
As if it had slipped from a wandering star;
And all through the night came the weird refrain,
Like a moan from the dying who die in pain.

The morning dawned, and the east wind blew
Icy and fierce, and came whistling through
The crannies and chinks of window and door,
And lifted the carpet upon the floor;
But the gladdening light of a new sunrise
Brought a sense of relief to long watching eyes.

Then tidings came, like a terrible blight,
Of the wreck of a ship in the dark, dark night,
As at anchor it lay in a sheltered bay,
At the close of the stormy yesterday;
Securely there, she rolled and heaved
On the moving tide—none aboard believed
Or dreamt of danger, as lulled to sleep
On the restless waves so blue and deep.
How little they thought that their eyes no more
Would raptured gaze on their own dear shore.

A steam ship came in the dead of the night,
And struck her a terrible blow. In spite
Of the guns, and the cries, and signs of distress,
They sank and they sank—and then they press
To the rigging and cling. A lady there
With glittering jewels and streaming hair
Held fast, but at last in her faint despair
Her fingers loosed, she was seen to glide
And sink in the yeasty yawning tide.

The sun shone out on the terrible scene
Of havoc and loss, where yester e'en
Were a thousand emigrants, women and men,
Happy, and hopeful, and joyous, when
Suddenly, awfully, some asleep,
Were cast on the breast of the merciless deep,
Whose wild waves rushing with crests of snow,
Kept tossing their victims to and fro,
And laid them in order along the shore,
Long lines of corpses—what more? yea more.

See there, where the tide in a nook makes swirl,
Was found the form of a fair young girl,

With long bright tresses of golden hair:
She seemed, like a delicate sea weed, where
The pearly shells were wreathed and twined.
Like the coral around her neck, and inclined
Us to think that this terrible scene on the wave,
Was a wreck and a sack of a mermaid's cave.

  *   *   *   *

O, when will the spirit of wisdom teach,
Or justice stern make punishment reach,
Those desperate men, who are ever at strife
With the ocean; yet reckless of human life?
The signs of the times they might well discern,
And the dullest of dullards of captains learn,
That he who imperils a life at sea,
Imperils his own, or his liberty:
And will from THE SERVICE ROLL have erased
A name degraded—a man disgraced.

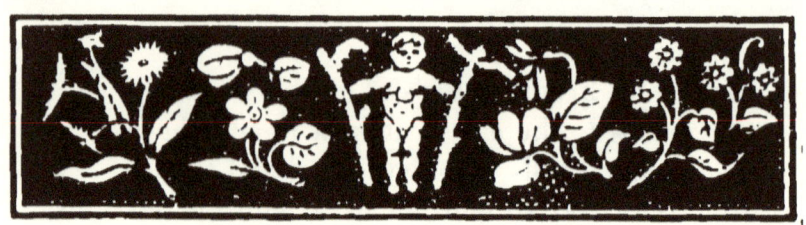

THE FOUNDLING.

THIS is a tale of simple pathos, told
With unpremeditated eloquence,
Of one whose life's devotion is a type
Of many lives in this our island home.
With meek, appealing eyes and
trem'lous voice,
She poured her story in the listening ear
Of one whose open hand and generous heart
Were never closed against the voice of woe.

" Alone, alone! I feel I am alone,
A homeless one amid a crowd of homes,
A stranger in a city filled with life.
Alone, alone! 'tis sad to be alone,
A poor, a solitary, nameless thing,
A sheaf of sea-weed floating on the wave,
A wingèd seed borne by the breezy air,
Knowing not whence I came, nor where my rest.
I only know that here my lot is cast,
And here a transitory home I find,
Where I may linger peacefully awhile,
And hope to find a sphere of usefulness,
Where I may minister to ailing ones;
And through the open lips of spirit wounds

Instil the consolation that I need
To satisfy the longing of my soul!
Here every fibre of my eager heart
Expanding, touches beings like myself,
Lonely and desolate—as indeed I am!

"Think not I murmur at my dreary lot,
Or voice a single word complainingly.
No! Providence is kind, and grateful I
Will be for ever more to those whose hearts
Were stirred by truest impulse to provide
For those to whom earth's holiest name's denied.
But, oh my hunger for a place called home!
The yearning throbbings for a mother's breast
On which to lay my weary head and rest!

"The tenderest name my lips have ever named,
Is Friend! The more endearing, fonder names
Of Father, Mother, I have never known;
Nor home, nor kindred none; nor ever shall.
But this I know, my gracious God is good,
And all my aim in life is to administer
To those who suffer, all the good I can.
From kindly, alien hearts I have received
The love that swells my own; to such I give
In gratitude the service of my life.
And if no parent smiles to urge me on,
'Tis sweet to feel that some will deign to cheer
With gentle words the lonely Foundling's heart,
And strew some blossoms on her rugged way!
O! He Who rules the destiny of all,
Will be my guide through all life's perils here:
I trust my conscience will approve my deeds,
And all my actions be approved on high.

"Could men but feel the joy soft accents give!
Could all but feel—I know indeed *you* do—
The soothing balm a gentle word supplies
To my poor heart, and hear my prayers ascend
For you and such as you. I sleep, I dream,
And waking find my dreams have been of you
Whose names I murmur even when I sleep;
The open ear that hears the orphan's cry,
The loving heart that fosters friendless ones,
The great All Good that made and governs all,
Will listen to the Foundling's earnest prayer,
And pour upon your hallowed, loving lives
The bounteous recompense your deeds deserve."

He heard no more, but gently loosed the hand
So closely clasped, and silent turned away!

WORDS.

"Words, Words, Words." HAMLET.

WORDS! wondrous words! so fine, so full of power
    To soothe or thrill the heart's vibrating chords.
    Man's brain's a crucible where, hour by hour,
The golden thought's transmuted into words!
For noblest WORD! is purest, loftiest thought,
To faultless form and perfect utterance wrought!

The quickening Voice that spoke mankind at first!
    Had earlier pierced the dark chaotic night,
Where earth for countless ages had been nursed,
    And bade it roll in beauty into light;
The MASTER's word infolds the MASTER's will
'Tis heard: winds cease, and raging seas are still.

The Great High Priest, Creator, God of all,
    The Voice paternal, Eden's garden walked,
Taught man his speech, that man on Him might call,
    Then God and man like friends familiar talked.
But pitying Heaven soon man a rebel saw—
God veiled, but spake, the Word became our law.

WORDS.

Some words are weak, however loud their tone!
    Some words potential, though in whispers given,
By gentlest forces Nature's power is shown,
    As rocks by gliding streams are rent and riven.
The mightiest power is viewless, but increases
From hour to hour, till all obstruction ceases.

All thoughts are pure to those who purely think;
    All words are true to those who truly read;
Truth's well is clear to all who clearly drink;
    And man must reap whate'er he sows as seed!
From minds corrupt, corrupting thoughts will flow,
As stagnant pools must poisonous herbage show.

Though words be air, and air the softest breath
    That bears the summer perfumes in its breeze,
One word may rouse and fling with arrowy scath
    The whirling light—make wild the slumbering seas:
Hot, seething, furious, fuming, chafes the main!
Another word—and all is peace again.

The first great words were uttered, Light and Life,
    With second words came Charity and Love;
The third, to come through death, relieves from strife,
    And conquering leads to angel homes above.
From pain, from care, from every peril free.
Around its brow the wreath of victory!

The great Omniscient fills the teeming earth,
    His beauty seen, His voice controlling heard
From myriad tongues, of low or lofty birth.

Hearts throb, eyes glisten, when the soul is stirred
By men inspired, who speak in words of flame
What all have felt, but only they could frame.

When close tumultuous numbers madly pressed,
    The patriot poet calmly stood on high;
Stretched forth his hand, laid bare his manly breast,
    While fury flashed from many a frenzied eye.
His voice prevailed, the murderous myriads swayed,
Spellbound, they listened, melted, and obeyed!

The craven crowd before the tumult fled,
    One man alone stood firm—his weapon *words*.
Amazed, they halted, cheered him as a god,
    Threw up their caps, and sheathed their thirsty swords.
Such marvellous power rebellious France has seen,
And such thy deathless glory, *Lamartine!*

Despise not words, the garments of the soul;
· One thoughtless word may bring an age of pain.
Words once let fall defy thy vain control,
    They work their work, but will return again
To bless, or curse, the tongue that gave them life.
Watch well thy tongue, and keep thyself from strife.

Words! wondrous words! so fine, so full of power
    To soothe or thrill the heart's vibrating chords.
Man's brain's a crucible where, hour by hour,
    The golden thought's transmuted into words!
For noblest WORD! is purest, loftiest thought
To faultless form and perfect utterance wrought!

MY BOOKS.

I LOVE my books as drunkards love their wine;
The more I drink, the more they seem divine;
With joy elate my soul in love runs o'er,
And each fresh draught is sweeter than before!
Books bring me friends where'er on earth I be,
Solace of solitude,—bonds of society!

I love my books! they are companions dear,
Sterling in worth, in friendship most sincere;
Here talk I with the wise in ages gone,
And with the nobly gifted of our own:
If love, joy, laughter, sorrow please my mind,
Love, joy, grief, laughter in my books I find.

LYRICS, SONGS, AND SONNETS.

> "Ev'n then a wish (I mind its power),
> A wish that to my latest hour
>   Shall strongly heave my breast,
> That I for poor auld Scotland's sake,
> Some usefu' plan or beuk could make,
>   Or sing a song at least."
>   BURNS.

HAST THOU A FRIEND?

Hast thou a friend? Oh hold him fast,
    Fling not his hand away;
Thou of a treasure art possessed
    Thou'lt find not every day:
Oh let no hasty word or look,
Blot out his name from memory's book.

A Friend! to man the noblest gift
    That Heaven has in its power:
Stronger than death, and yet, most strange,
    More frail than feeblest flower:
For that which braved the storm severe,
May yet be blighted by a sneer!

He may have errors; who has not?
    Who dares perfection claim?
God gave thy friend some worthy parts,
    Fix all thy heart on them.
His virtues rightly drawn—I ween
His faults in shade will not be seen.

If thou would'st keep thy friend thine own,
    Be open, be sincere;

What thou unto thyself art known,
    Such to thy friend appear;
'Twixt him and thee have no disguise;
In this true friendship's secret lies.

Thou *hast* a friend! oh hold him fast;
    Fling not his hand away;
Thou of a treasure art possessed
    That's found not every day;
Oh let no hasty word, or look,
Blot thy friend's name from thy heart's book!

1847.

WHO DARES TO SCORN?

WHO dares to scorn the meanest
    thing,
  The humblest weed that grows,
  While pleasure spreads its joyous
    wing
On every breeze that blows!
The simplest flower that hidden blooms,
  The lowliest on the ground,
Is lavish of its rare perfumes,
  And scatters sweetness round.

The poorest friend upholds a part
  Of life's harmonious plan;
The weakest hand may have the art
  To serve the strongest man;
The bird that highest, clearest sings
  To greet the morning's birth,
Falls down to drink, with folded wings,
  Love's rapture on the earth.

From germs too small for mortal sight
  Grow all things that are seen;
The floating particles of light
  Weave nature's robe of green;

The motes that fill the sunny rays
    Build ocean, earth and sky—
The wondrous orbs that round us blaze
    Are motes to Deity.

Life, love, devotion, closely twine
    Like tree, and flower, and fruit—
They ripen by a power divine,
    Are fed by leaf and root.
The man who would be truly great
    Must venture to be small:
On airy columns rests the dome
    That shining circles all.

Small duties grow to mighty deeds;
    Small words to thoughts of power;
Great forests spring from tiny seeds,
    As moments make the hour;
And life—howe'er it lowly grows,
    The essence to it given;
Like odour from the breathing rose,
    Floats evermore to heaven.

1854.

MAY-DAY.

Invocation.

THE biting wintry winds are laid,
   And spring comes carolling o'er
      the earth;
   Mead, mountain, glen, and forest
      glade
Are ringing with melodious mirth.
The fields have doffed their sober brown,
   And donned their robes of lovely green,
On level mead, on breezy down,
   Are flowers in countless myriads seen.
      Come forth, come forth, enjoy the day,
      And welcome song-inspiring May!

Through bud and branch, and gnarled trunk,
   To deepest root, when quickening light
Touches the torpid juices, sunk
   In slumber by the winter's might,
Electric currents tingling rise,
   Each circle swells with life anew:

Wide opening to the sunny skies,
  Young grateful blossoms drink the dew.
    Come forth, time-furrowed age, and say
    If anything feels old in May?

Step o'er the brook, climb up the bank,
  And peep beneath those withered leaves—
Among the roots with wild weeds rank;
  See how the pregnant earth upheaves
With pulsing life! How quiveringly
  The timid young flowers, blushing, bend
Their gentle heads, where modesty
  And all the graces sweetly blend.
    Come forth, come forth, ye young, and say
    What cheeks can vie with rosy May?

From desk and 'Change come forth and range;
  From clanging forge, and shop, and mill;
From crowded room, from board and loom,
  Come! bid the rattling wheels be still.
Come, old and young, come, strong and weak,
  Indulge the limb and brain with rest.
Come, gushing youth and wrinkled cheek,
  In leisure feel your labour blest.
    Come forth, come forth, and hail the day.
    Come, welcome in the glorious May!

Come, ere the dappled East has burned—
  Made molten gold the winding stream;
Come, ere the fiery sun has turned
  The pearly dew to misty steam;
Come, ere the lark has left his nest,
  Or lambkin bleated on the hill;

Come, see how nature looks in rest,
  And learn the bliss of being still.
    Come forth, come forth, and hail the day!
    Come, welcome blossom-teeming May!

Æolian murmurs swell the breeze,
  Enchant the ear, and charm the brain;
While merry bells and humming bees
  Fill up the burden of the strain.
On earth, in air, oh, everywhere,
  A brighter glory shines to-day;
Old bards reveal how birds prepare
  New songs to herald joyous May.
    Come forth, come forth, nor lingering stay,
    Come, crown with flowers the matchless May!

CONSUMMATION.

No trumpet's thrilling call is heard
  To servile host or lordly crest,
But that mysterious, viceless word,
  By which the world is onward prest—
Which bids the grass in beauty grow,
  And stars their path of glory keep,
Makes winds and waves harmonious flow,
  And dreaming infants smile in sleep.
    That voice, resistless in its sway,
    Turns winter wild to flowery May.

From edges of the dusky shade,
  That canopies the restless town,
Come trooping many a youth and maid,
  With flushing face and tresses brown.

High hopes have they, their hearts to please.
   They seek the wild wood's haunted dell:
They laughing come, by twos and threes,
     But chiefly twos. I mark them well—
        So trimly drest, so blithe and gay,
        With them it seems 'tis always May.

They steep their kerchiefs in the dew;
   Then follow wondrous wringings out:
As wingèd seeds were blown, they knew
   What laggard lovers were about.
Some pluck the glowing leaves to learn
   If love declared be love sincere;
Or in red ragged streaks discern
   Love lost, and virtue's burning tear.
      Oh, love is earnest though in play,
      When comes the love-inciting May.

With hawthorn blooms and speckled shells,[1]
   Chaplets are twined for blushing brows;
While gipsies work their magic spells,
   And lovers pledge their deathless vows.
Then round and round with many a bound,
   They tread the mystic fairy ring.
The silent woods have voices found,
   And echoing chorus while they sing:
      "With shout and song, and dance and play,
      We welcome in the peerless May!"

---

[1] In some parts of the north of England they form chaplets for May-day with flowers and speckled shells of eggs, as here described.

Linked hand in hand, their tripping feet
  Keep time to mirth's inspiring voice:
They wheel and meet, advance, retreat,
  Till happy hearts in love rejoice.
The ring is formed for kisses sly—
  Leaping and racing o'er the plain;
The young wish time would quicker fly,
  The old wish they were young again.
    Away with care: no cares to-day!
    Care slumbers on the lap of May!

The voice that bade them welcome forth,
  Now gently, kindly whispers "Home!"
To-day has been a day of mirth,
  To-morrow sterner duties come.
Such pleasures nerve the arm for strife,
  Bring joyous thoughts and golden dreams,
To mingle with the web of life—
  And memory store with woods and streams.
    Such joys drive cankering care away;
    Then ever welcome, flowery May!

May 1. 1852.

LIFE.

IFE ever striving, restless, and driving,
    All is mysterious: who shall decide
Which is the best, labour or rest?
    Pleasures are bubbles that float on its tide;
Glancing and gleaming, beautiful seeming,
    Touch them they vanish, and where have they flown?
Where? ah where? They have melted in air,
    And hearts they had gladden'd are weeping alone.

Patiently ever Time mingles together
    The idle, the vain, and the workers for bread,
Sighing or singing, merry bells ringing,
    And blending with others that toll for the dead!
Pomp and perplexity, wealth and adversity,
    Jumble and jostle their way in the street;
Ease and anxiety, want and satiety,
    Weave them a woof that is never complete!

Listless, repining, worthless and whining,
    Many of life make a wretched display;
While health with its treasures, and youth with its pleasures
    Can nestle and laugh among sweet-scented hay.

Toiling or playing admit no delaying—
   Earnest in everything, such be our plan :
Faithful, confiding—a friend's errors hiding !
   Making of all things the best that we can.

Some may despise life ! Folly defies life !
   O cherish it dearly, for brief is its stay !
Stand to it bravely, joyfully, gravely,
   Life is a game that is pleasant to play !
And when all is over, around us may hover
   Angel bands singing " 'Tis fading away,"
The wounded heart healing and gently revealing
   A life without sorrow—Eternal the day.

1858.

MANSFIELD.[1]

DOWN the Nith a stranger came,
    Un-tamped with title, birth, or fame:
    A Poet's warmth his only claim
        To halt a while at Mansfield:
He came by hills high, bleak, and bare;
So crisp and clear the autumn air,
A charm to banish every care
        Was found at pleasant Mansfield.

Though morning skies looked leaden grey,
The drizzling mist soon rolled away,
And only brighter left the day,
        That smiling shone on Mansfield.
So high among the mountains placed,
Reclaimed with skill, adorned with taste,
A garden conquered from the waste,
        An Eden made of Mansfield.

O'er Corsoncon the winds may sweep
With freezing breath when snow lies deep:

---

[1] The residence of Sir James Stuart Menteth, Bart., near New Cumnock, Ayrshire.

But desolating storms must keep
    Their circuit wide of Mansfield:
The birds that fly before the gale,
Instinctive seek the sheltered vale,
And find—when other haunts may fail—
    A safe retreat at Mansfield.

O may the streamlet bubbling near
Dance on for ever brisk and clear,
To please the eye and charm the ear
    Of all who stay at Mansfield!
O who could help but love the place
Where Art with Nature blent we trace;
Though most we love the gentle grace
    That meets a friend at Mansfield.

Yet, eyes untrained may fail to see
In hill and glen, in stream and tree,
The beauty all so plain to me
    When wandering over Mansfield;
For judgment, ruled by sight alone,
Detects no fire within the stone,
Nor in the string the melting tone
    That thrills the heart at Mansfield.

As mountain torrents, rushing by,
Make smooth the rocks that in them lie;
So time refineth lineage high—
    The Princely line of Mansfield.
While seasons, years, and cycles roll,
And crowd with change Time's awful scroll,
May there be found a kindly soul
    To rule the house of Mansfield!

False friends turn base when fortune frowns:
Mean man his brother man disowns;
Misfortune like a halo crowns
      The brows of man at Mansfield.
When losses sear, and men oppress;
And sorrow follows deep distress,
If honour lives, the warm caress
      Is ne'er denied at Mansfield.

The stranger gone no more may view
Those gables quaint, that ancient yew,
Nor odorous flowers of every hue
      That belt with blossom Mansfield.
Like them his eyes with dew may fill,
And sympathetic tears distil;
But neither time nor space can chill
      His memory of Mansfield.

1859.

MY BONNIE WEE WIFIE.

Y bonnie wee wifie, I'm waefu' to
leave thee,
To leave thee sae lanely an' far frae
me ;
Come night and come morning,
I'll soon be returning,
Then, oh my dear wifie, how happy we'll be !
Oh, cauld is the night, and the way dreigh an'
dreary,
The snaw's drifting blindly o'er moorland an' lea;
All nature looks eerie ; how can she be cheery ?
Since weel she maun ken I am parted frae thee !

Oh, wae is the lammie that's lost its dear mammie,
An' waefu' the bird that sits chirping alane ;
The plaints they are making, their wee bit hearts
breaking,
Are throbbings o' pleasure compared wi' my pain.
The sun to the simmer, the bark to the timmer,
The sense to the saul, an' the light to the e'e,
The bud to the blossom, sae thou'rt to my bosom ;
Oh, wae's my heart wifie, when parted frae thee!

There's nae guid availing in weeping or wailing,
  Should frien'ship be failing wi' fortune's decay!
Love in our hearts glowing, its riches bestowing,
  Bequeaths us a treasure man takes not away.
Let nae anxious feeling creep o'er thy heart, stealing
  The bloom frae thy cheek, when thou'rt thinking of me.
Come night and come morning, I'll then be returning,
  Nae mair cozie wifie we parted shall be.

1843.

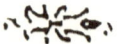

A THOUGHT.

MEN'S lives like waves in quick succession rise,
  And heave, and roll, and break upon the shore;
    Youth follows childhood, manhood follows youth,
Old age succeeds, then death, and all is o'er!

Or, like the peals of some far-distant bell,
  Knell follows knell, and chime succeeds to chime.
Death follows life,—life ever springs from death:
  Thus endlessly revolves the chain of Time!

OUR WEDDING DAY.

Dear Wife:—

SINCE six-and-thirty years ago,
What surging tides of joy and woe
Have passed o'er us, we only know!

Whilst old friends fade, new friends arise;
What shadowy gloom, what sunny skies,
Alternate pass before our eyes!

Yet sweet birds sing as then they sang;
The wild flowers spring as then they sprang;
And joy bells ring as then they rang!

Grey hairs may glisten, where of yore
Dark tresses waved thy temples o'er—
But yet I love thee more and more.

For more and more, to soul and sense
Have ripened all those virtues, whence
Come all my love of life intense!

And now whilst seated side by side,
Thou'rt still my blessing and my pride,
Far more than when thou wert my bride.

It may be that our eyes grow dim—
What matter if before them swim
Angelic visions bright of Him!

Of Christ, in whom all love we trace,
The perfect model of our race
Who beckons us! And face to face

When we shall meet Him, may it be
That we shall all His Glory see,
And hear Him welcome thee and me!

And with that welcome, hand in hand,
May we as bride and bridegroom stand,
Co-heirs of all that happy land!

1874.

TOGETHER.

A SONG.

TOGETHER, dearest, we have played,
   As girl and boy together;
Through storm and calm, in sun
    and shade,
   In spring or wintry weather.
Oh! every pang that stinging came
   But made our love the dearer;
If danger lowered—'twas all the same,
   We only clung the nearer.

In riper years, when all the world
   Lay bathed in light before us,
And life in rainbow hues unfurled
   Its glowing banner o'er us,
Amid the beauty storms would rise
   And flowers collapsing wither,
And open friends turn hidden foes,
   Yet were we blest together.

But now the battle's fought and won,
   And care with life is flying,

While, setting slowly like the sun,
    Ambition's fires are dying,
We gather hope with fading strength,
    And go, we know not whither,
Contented if in death at last
    We sleep in peace together.

1856.

LOVE AND BEAUTY.

WHEN fairest things of earth become,
    Then nearer they approach decay:
Death hides him in their freshest bloom,
They bud, bloom, wither, in a day
The flower falls, its hues are gone,
The fragrance of its life lives on.

I thought that Beauty was Love's shrine,
    That lips, cheeks, eyes, and motion were
Its ministers, themselves divine:
    They faded, still *Love* lingered there!
Youth, Strength, and Beauty quickly fly,
Love's essence lives and cannot die!

OUR SHIP.[1]

SONG, a song, brave hearts, a song
    To the ship in which we ride;
That bears us along right gallantly,
    Defying both time and tide.
Away, away, by night and day,
    Propelled by steam and wind;
The watery waste before her lies,
    And a flaming wake behind.
    Then a ho and a hip, to the gallant ship,
        That carries us o'er the sea,
    Through storm and foam, to a western home—
        A home of the brave and free.

With a fearless bound to the depths profound,
    She rushes with proud disdain;
While pale lips tell the fears that swell,
    Lest she never should rise again.

---

[1] Written on board the Cunard steamer "Niagara," and set to music by Mr. Hatton, who was a fellow-passenger, and sung with much success by him in his professional tour in the United States.

With a courser's pride, she paws the tide,
  Unbridled by bit I trow;
While the churlish sea she dashes with glee,
  In a cataract from her prow.
    Then a ho and a hip, to the gallant ship,
      That carries us o'er the sea,
    Through storm and foam, to a western home—
      A home of the brave and free.

She bears not on board a lawless horde,
  Piratic in thought and deed;
Yet the sword they would draw in defence of law,
  In the nation's hour of need:
Professors and poets, and merchantmen,
  Whose voyagings never cease,
From shore to shore, the wide world o'er;
  Their bonds are the bonds of peace.
    Then a ho and a hip, to the gallant ship,
      That carries us o'er the sea,
    Through storm and foam, to a western home—
      A home of the brave and free.

She boasts the brave, the dutiful,
  The aged and the young;
And woman bright and beautiful,
  And childhood's prattling tongue.
With a dip and a rise, like a bird she flies,
  And we fear not the storm or squall;
For faithful officers guide the helm,
  And heaven protects us all.
    Then a ho and a hip, to the gallant ship,
      That carries us o'er the sea,
    Through storm and foam, to a western home—
      A home of the brave and free.

1848.

TRUTH AND HONOUR.

A SONG FOR ALL SEASONS.

IF wealth thou art wooing, or title, or fame,
There is that in the doing, brings honour or shame;
There is something in running life's perilous race,
Will stamp thee as worthy, or brand thee as base:
    Oh, then be a MAN, and whatever betide,
    Keep TRUTH thy companion, and HONOUR thy guide.

If a king, be thy kingship right royally shown,
And trust to thy subjects to shelter thy throne:
Rely not on weapons, or armies of might,
But on that which endureth—laws, loving and right;
    Though a KING be a MAN, and whatever betide,
    Keep TRUTH thy companion, and HONOUR thy guide.

If a noble, remember though ancient thy blood,
The heart truly noble, is that which is good;

Should a stain of dishonour encrimson thy brow
Thou art slave to the peasant that sweats at the
    plough:
  Be NOBLE as MAN, and whatever betide,
  Keep TRUTH thy companion, and HONOUR
    thy guide.

If a husband, or lover, be faithful and kind,
For doubting is death, to the sensitive mind;
Love's exquisite passion a breath may destroy:
Who soweth in faith reapeth harvests of joy.
  Love dignifies man, and whatever betide,
  Keep TRUTH thy companion, and HONOUR
    thy guide.

If a father, be firm, yet forgiving; and prove
How the child honours him who rebuketh in love;
If rich, or if poor—or whate'er thou mayst be,
Remember, the *truthful* alone are the *free*.
  Erect in thy manhood—whatever betide,
  Keep TRUTH thy companion, and HONOUR
    thy guide.

Then, though sickness may come, and misfortune
    may fall,
There is that in thy bosom surviveth them all;
TRUTH—HONOUR—LOVE—FRIENDSHIP, no tem-
    pests can pale,
They are beacons of light in adversity's gale.
  Oh, the MANLIKE is GODLIKE, no ill shall
    betide,
  While TRUTH's thy companion and HONOUR
    thy guide.

THE LIME-TREE.

SING, sing the Lime—the odorous Lime!
   With tassels of gold and leaves so green.
   It ever has made the pleasantest shade
For lovers to loiter and talk unseen—
When high overhead its arms are spread,
   And bees are busily buzzing around,
When sunlight and shade a woof have laid
   Of flickering net-work on the ground.
   I love the Lime—the odorous Lime!
     With tassels of gold and leaves so green:
   To its balmy bower in the noontide hour
     Is wafted pleasure on wings unseen.

When the Switzer fought, and gallantly wrought
   His charter of freedom with bow and spear,
A branch was torn from the Lime, and borne
   As the patriot's hope and the tyrant's fear.
They proudly tell where the herald youth fell
   With the living branch in his dying hand.
Blood-hallowed the tree is of liberty—
   The sacred symbol in Switzerland.

THE LIME-TREE.

    O the Lime—the odorous Lime!
      With tassels of gold, and leaves so green;
    The whisperings heard when its leaves are
        stirred
      Are the voices of martyrs that prompt
        unseen.

I love it the more for the days of yore,
  And the avenue leading—I tell not where;
But, there was a bower, and a witching flower
  Of gracefullest beauty grew ripening there.
From valley and hill, from forge and mill,
  From neighbouring hamlets murmurs stole;
But the sound most dear to my sensitive ear
  Was a musical whisper that thrilled my soul.
    O the Lime—the odorous Lime!
      With tassels of gold and leaves so green:
    It ever has made the pleasantest shade
      For lovers to wander and woo unseen.

When the garish noon had passed, and the moon
  Came silvering forest, and lake, and tower,
In the hush of the night, so calm and bright,
  How silent and sweet was the Linden bower.
They may boast of their forests of larch and pine,
  Of maple and elm, and scented thorn,
Of ash and of oak, defying the stroke
  Of the tempest on pinions of fury borne:
    Give me the Lime—the odorous Lime!
      With tassels of gold and leaves so green;
    The vows that are made beneath its shade
      Are throbbings of spirits that bless unseen.

WOLLATON HALL, 1851.

SONG.

SING, lady, sing—and only sing
  The song you sing so well:
Its touching strains sweet raptures
    bring,
  And bind me with their spell:
Enrapt, I nothing seem to hear
  Beyond the sweet refrain,
Embracing all the heart holds dear:
  So sing that song again.

Another song I hoped to hear
  Whose cadence low and deep,
Might well a fainting spirit cheer,
  Then soothe the soul in sleep!
It may not be! Then sing for me
  That touching dear refrain,
Which stirs the heart tumultuously,
  Sing—sing that song again!

1874.

LONDON.[1]

IF glorious deeds deserve a song,
    Then, London, one to thee!
Thy ancient name all tongues proclaim
    The watchword of the Free:
Where'er the flag of liberty
    Is righteously unfurl'd,
There London is;—her mighty heart
    Beats through the civil world.
    Then ho! for London, brave and high,
        So shall she ever be,
    While Justice rules within her walls,
        And Honour guides the Free.

Of conquering Peace the pioneers
    Her dauntless merchants are;
Their ships are found the world around,
    Her sons 'neath every star.
Her sheltering tree of Liberty
    Spreads hourly more and more;
Its roots run under every sea,
    It blooms on every shore.

---

[1] Written for the occasion of the Queen's visit to the City in 1851.

Unfading youth, untarnished truth,
    Great London! bide with thee;
Of cities, Queen, supreme, serene,
    The leader of the Free.

In days of dread, she boldly stood
    Undaunted, though alone,
To guard with might the people's right
    Invaded by the Throne;
And yet when civil fury raged,
    And Loyalty took wing,
Her gallant bands, with bows and brands,
    Defended well their king.
        Then ho! for London, Might and Right,
            With her, twin brothers be:
        To curb with Right the despot Might,
            Exalting still the Free!

The weak, deposed, discrowned King!
    The Patriot brave exiled,
Alike have here a refuge found,
    Where Freedom ever smiled:
And evermore she spreads her store,
    The exile to maintain,
And what has been her pride before,
    Shall be her boast again.
        Then ho! for London, Ward and Guard
            To all who shelter seek:
        A terror to the tyrant strong,
            A succour to the weak.

And now within her ancient Halls,
    Where Freemen ever stand,

She welcomes men from every clime,
  With open heart and hand;
She welcomes men of every creed,
  The brave, the wise, the good;
And bids all nations form indeed
  A loyal brotherhood.
    Clasped hand in hand let every land
      Like loving brothers be;
    From pole to pole, let every soul
      United be—and free.

FIRST VERSES IN AN ALBUM.

JUDITH! I've watched thy joyous ways,
  All clear as mountain brook is;
Thy life's young leaf, as free from grief,
  Unspotted as this book is!
And I would pray, it ever may
  Escape Time's touch of rudeness;
Till every page from youth to age
  Is written o'er with goodness.

Around thy heart keep closely twined
  All warm and kind affections;
And cherish ever in thy mind
  The sweetest recollections.
Whilst opening, ripening day by day,
  In mental power and beauty;
Let Knowledge light the lamp of Faith,
  And gild the path of duty.

1848.

THE SWITZER'S SONG ON THREATENED INVASION.

I.

HE gusty wind of stormy March
    Comes booming loudly through the trees;
From dusky pine and lofty larch,
    Ring wild and weird-like harmonies.
With dreary moan or startling shriek,
    It whirling smites our cottage grey,
Then fearless leapeth gorge and peak,
    Till, passion spent, it dies away.
      Pile high the faggots! let them blaze—
      A beacon light to lands astray:
      With generous wine the flagon fill!
        Through storms and tears
        Hope radiant peers:
      Life's short—enjoy it while you may!

II.

O'er all the East a tempest lowers,
    Scared Freedom turns to face the gloom,

Such stillness leads the thunder showers,
  Or hurrying march of fierce simoom.
The surging sounds from gathering hosts
  Float hitherward, like ocean's hum.
We fear no foe—the nations know
  The Switzers' welcome when they come.
    Pile high the faggots! let them blaze!
      Bring forth the trusty sword and gun!
    With generous wine the flagon fill!
        Come hope or fear,
        Our course is clear—
    Life's short, but sweet with duty done!

III.

Should ruthless squadrons venture near
  With flame of war—however brave—
Our shaggy trees shall form their bier—
  Our valleys green provide a grave.
Here thrice ten thousand hearts beat high,
  To guard the land they love so well;
Willing great Arnold's death to die;—
  Worthy the bow of dauntless Tell.
    Pile high the faggots! let them blaze!
      'Tis wise preparing for the worst.
    With generous wine the flagon fill!
        Come peace or war,
        Come death or scar—
    Life's short, and should be duly nursed

IV.

The storm that strikes the pampered elm,
  And brings its crown of glory low,
While wrestling with our mountain pine
  Makes every root the firmer grow.

Though tyrants strain, with rack and chain,
  Till beaded blood tears start and roll—
O Torture's tooth but graves the truth
  The deeper in the patriot's soul.
    Pile high the faggots! let them blaze!
      The voice of freedom swells the gale:
    With generous wine the flagon fill!
      The God of might
      Defends the right—
    Life's short, but none dare us assail.

v.

For liberty our fathers fought,
  For liberty we'll fight again.
Better is death with freedom wrought,
  Than life where liberty is slain.
If poor in wealth, we're rich in health;
  If small our power, few cares have we.
Within our misty mountain home,
  We're, like our Alpine torrents, free.
    Pile high the faggots! let them blaze!
      Our love of freedom ne'er shall cease;
    With generous wine the flagon fill!
      Come storm or strife—
      Come death or life,
    Rejoice, for heaven is full of peace!

1854.

PAST AND PRESENT.

AN OLD MAN'S SONG.

BRING hither—bring hither, the foam-
    ing jug,
  Creamy and spicy and steaming hot;
Now, we are slippered and warm and
    snug,
  Let the winds revel around our cot.
We'll summon the pleasures of years agone,
  And banish our presence all trial and strife;
No sorrow dare enter when we are alone,
  To dim with its shadow the joy of life.
    A liberal measure we'll fill, and drink
      To all who may love us, and we love well;
    O break not a bead on the glancing brink,
      A friendly spirit in each may dwell.

At starting, how sunny and warm our days,
  How joyous the breezes around us blew!
The earth with beauty,—the air with praise
  Were filled, and nothing but love we knew.

When vapours the changeable West[1] had nursed,
    Came wreathing cloudily, darkly down,
How little I heeded the storm that burst.—
    The face of my wife never wore a frown.
        A liberal measure I'll fill, and drink
            To her, the devoted, who loves so well.
        I'll break not a bead on the glancing brink,
            But fancy her spirit in each may dwell.

With vanishing clouds came raptures new,
    Our wealth of pleasure eclipsed our care;
Time hurried, but clustering round us grew
    Fair beings, who shouting made music rare.
Strong, healthy, and honest—our God we thank!
For Polly and Lizzie, and Meggie so sly,
For saucy Willie, and Tom and Frank—
    O bless them, they never have cost a sigh!
        A liberal measure we'll fill, and drink
            To the darlings who love us, and we love well.
        Nor break we a bead on the glancing brink,
            Their spirit of duty in each may dwell.

All mated, and flitted, and dwelling apart,
    With boys and girls, a dozen or more—
Though absent they're present and near our heart,
    For them there is honour and love in store.
How happy this boisterous Christmas Eve,
    Are all who are able to spend it thus;

---

[1] The American panic, 1856.

Though lonely, we feel not alone, nor grieve—
  Our children's blessings encircle us.
    In honour of all who love us well,
      No more we will measure the beaded wine,
    But pray, that in each and all may dwell
      The spirit that made our Lord divine.

1856.

FLORENCE NIGHTINGALE.

WITH lofty song we love to cheer
  The hearts of daring men;
Applauded thus, they gladly hear
  The trumpet's call again.
But now we sing of lowly deeds
  Devoted to the brave,
Where she, who stems the wound that bleeds,
  A hero's life may save:
And heroes saved exulting tell
  How well her voice they knew;
How sorrow near it could not dwell,
  But spread its wings and flew.

Neglected, dying in despair,
  They lay till woman came,
To soothe them with her gentle care,
  And feed life's flickering flame.
When wounded sore, on fever's rack,
  Or cast away as slain,
She called their fluttering spirits back,
  And gave them strength again.

"We might not always see the face,
  Which suffering could dispel:
But we could turn and kiss the place
  On which her shadow fell." [1]

When words of wroth profaning rung,
  She moved with pitying grace;
Her presence stilled the wildest tongue,
  And holy [2] grew the place.
They knew that they were cared for then,
  Their eyes forgot their tears;
In dreamy sleep they lost their pain,
  And thought of early years—
Of early years, when all was fair,
  Of faces sweet and pale.
They woke: the angel bending there
  Was—Florence Nightingale!

1855.

Music by J. W. Hatton.

---

[1] "She would speak to one and to another, and nod and smile to many more, but she could not do it to all; but we could kiss her shadow as it fell, and lay our heads on the pillow again, content."—*Soldier's Letter from the Crimea.*

[2] "Before she came there was cussin' and swearin', but after that it was as holy as a church."

THE IRISH GLEANER.

THE DAWN OF A BRIGHTER DAY.

FROM the bustling east to the idle west—
    From the north to the southmost shore—
    O'er hill, through bog, in light and fog,
You may travel all Ireland o'er.
Where energy, liberty, love, were dead,
    Or in senseless stupor lay,
        Hope, smiling, beams,
        And its radiance streams
On the dawn of a brighter day.

The pestilence came like a quenchless flame
    On the breath of a poisonous wind;
You might reckon its force and track its course
    By the ruin it left behind:
Nor youth, nor beauty, nor sex was spared—
    Its mission was still to slay!
        From the desolate past
        There cometh at last
The dawn of a brighter day.

Though kindred led from kindred dead,
    They have found a home afar;
They have labour and rest in the beautiful west,
    Where trusty brethren are.
And those who remain in their own dear land
    While justice bears the sway—
        Have prosperous lives;
        For labour thrives
    In the dawn of a brighter day.

What matter, although the pauper's rags
    May flutter before the breeze!
Dead leaves are seen 'mid the living green
    Of the leafiest forest trees.
Though poverty lurks and beggary works,
    In the south, wherever we stray:
        Yet all around
        Is increasingly found
    The dawn of a brighter day.

Here many will find hearts warm and kind!
    Maids beautiful, lithe, and sweet—
You might envy the favoured grass they press
    In the tread of their naked feet!
A flood of melody swells the voice,
    And stealeth the soul away:
        'Tis beauty supreme
        Fulfilling the dream
    That told of a brighter day.

By head and hand, on sea and land,
    The present its future weaves;
By hill and plain, or where ears of grain
    Are gathered among the sheaves,

A spirit of love in labour lives,
  Bringing health and wealth away.
    The night has flown,
    The light has shone—
  'Tis the dawn of a brighter day!

1852.

SONG.

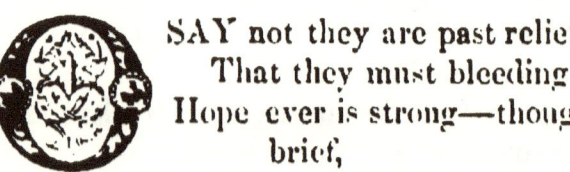

SAY not they are past relief,
  That they must bleeding die,
Hope ever is strong—though life is brief,
  So let me—let me try,
I pray thee LET ME TRY.[1]

I cannot bear their weary moan,
  Their piteous wailing cry;
'Tis wicked to leave them here alone—
  To save them let me try,
  In mercy LET ME TRY.

The heart was cheered—the hand was raised,
  Life's lustre filled the eye!
Their agony ceased—O God be praised,
  They let me—let me try—
  'TIS NEVER TOO LATE TO TRY!

1856.

---

[1] "Let me have these men—let me try to save them."—FLORENCE NIGHTINGALE, *Newspaper Report*.

EVA.

H slumber, my little one:
　　Sleep on my pretty one:
　　Smiles dream-awakened—are tokens
　　　　of bliss:
　　Delight never ceasing,
　But hourly increasing,—
What earthly enjoyment is equal to this?
　O Eva, sweet Eva, beautiful Eva,
My Eva, dear Eva, to fondle and kiss!

　　With winter winds blowing,
　　And winter clouds snowing,
There came to my arms a wee innocent dove;
　　My fever subduing,
　　My rapture renewing,
The child of my grief is a well-spring of love:
　O Eva, sweet Eva, beautiful Eva,
My Eva, dear Eva, my joy from above!

　　Her open lips breathing,
　　Sweet rosy smiles wreathing:—
Her cheek like the apple-bloom, pinky and fair;

  Her bonny blue eyes
  Are shreds filched from the skies;
And dusky as night is her wavy brow hair.
  O Eva, sweet Eva, beautiful Eva,
My Eva, dear Eva, my pride and my care!

  What clasping and clutching—
  Though aimless, how touching!
What fairy in whispering swells her young breast?
  Come close to my bosom,
  My blessing, my blossom;
Here! here's your home, darling, your refuge and rest.
  O Eva, sweet Eva, beautiful Eva,
My Eva, dear Eva, this, this is your nest!

  The trees gently waving,
  The lapping tide laving,
The streamlet from CLARAGH as glancing it ran,
  Had tongues to them given,
  Like music from heaven.
Repeating rejoicings awoke at Drishane.
  Oh Eva, sweet Eva, beautiful Eva,
My Eva, dear Eva, so pleasant to scan.

  Unbounded in measure,
  Sure Nature her treasure
Exhausted in moulding this baby of mine.
  Ye spirits of goodness,
  Defend her from rudeness!
Surround her, protect her, ye angels divine!
  O Eva, sweet Eva, beautiful Eva,
On thee may the sun of all blessedness shine!

  DRISHANE CASTLE, 1870.

MINNIE'S ISLE.

WHEN harvest glories crown the plain
With ripened fruit and golden grain,
Whilst sunshine falling bright and warm
Gives all the landscape double charm;
Where great trees wave and blossoms smile,
A dear retreat is Minnie's Isle.

From underneath the cedar's shade,
How sweet to view the glinting glade,
Where wychelms wave their branches wide,
Huge oaks and ashes side by side,
Like giants of the forest, pile
Their arms in guarding Minnie's Isle.

'Tis true no mountains lift on high
Their icy peaks, or pierce the sky.
Yet clouds like drifting hills of snow
Lie pictured in the lake below;
Whose dimpled wavelets all the while
Keep lapping—laving Minnie's Isle.

What joy when worldly woes oppress,
To seek this shady, cool recess;
To leave the turmoil, din, and strife,
The frettings of a restless life;
And for a season care beguile,
In musing here on Minnie's Isle.

Reposing here;—the poet's page
Restores to sense life's Golden Age;
Whilst mounting high on quivering wings,
The choiring lark melodious sings,
And pours on earth a heavenly wile,
To charm the ear on Minnie's Isle.

But who is Minnie? Who? Ah, there
A secret lies that few may share!
Suffice to know that in her face
We read each modest maiden grace.
Her voice? Is music!—And her smile?
Sheds light and life o'er Minnie's Isle.

Then see her flit from door to door,
To soothe, console, and cheer the poor,
Whose fervent daily prayers ascend
For her, their kind and gentle friend;
Thus love engenders love, and guile
No footing finds on Minnie's Isle.

All o'er the Minster's gladsome plain,
May virtue with contentment reign;
And if—as may—comes carking care,
May each, for each, a portion bear:
And nothing rough, or rude, or vile,
A shadow cast on Minnie's Isle.

But seasons pass, and changes come;
Now Minnie owns another home:
Another name dear Minnie bears,
With deeper joys, and wider cares.
On her and hers fair fortune smile,
Though far away from Minnie's Isle

August, 1873.

SONG.

MY dear Minnie mine—the dead leaves are falling,
   O dear Minnie mine—a spirit is calling,
I hear it—I feel it—it cannot be long,
Ere I with the angels will join in their song.
   O dear Minnie mine—sweet, sweet, Minnie mine!

My dear Minnie mine, as the spring-time grew olden;
O dear Minnie mine, when the autumn was golden,
Between came the summer and scattered the flowers,
Whilst Love with its rapture, dear Minnie, was ours,
   O dear Minnie mine—sweet, sweet, Minnie mine!

My dear Minnie mine, of the tender words spoken,
O dear Minnie mine, this—this is the token!

To know I must leave thee alone is deep sorrow,
Though dark be to-day!—it will brighten to-morrow,
    O dear Minnie mine—sweet, sweet, Minnie mine!

My dear Minnie mine—see the winter-clouds flying,
O dear Minnie mine—like the year I am dying,
Yet fervently pray that when this life is over,
My spirit still near thee may guardingly hover,
    O dear Minnie mine—sweet, sweet, Minnie mine!

1873.

"THE BUD IS ON THE BOUGH."

"THE bud is on the bough,
   And the blossom on the tree;"
But neither bud nor blossom bring
   A thrill of joy to me.
   Walled up within the city's gloom,
No pleasure can I know,
But like a caged linnet sing
   To chase away my woe!

The bud will grow a blossom,
   The blossom will grow pale,
And as it dies the fruit will spring,
   But fall when o'er the vale,
Stern Winter marches with his train
   In every wind that blows,
And I, unripe, with ripest fruit,
   May in the dust repose.

But Spring upon the seed will breathe
   The seed become a tree,
And on the tree so beautiful
   Will bud and blossom be:

And shall I know a second Spring?
  Yes! brighter far than they;
Where age puts on the blush of youth,
  And never more decay!

THE LILY OF THE VALLEY.

WHEN breezes bend the billowy grass,
  Each wave its flowery treasure shows,
While fitful storms that whirling pass
  Evolve the spirit of the rose;
Though crushed—returning good for ill—
  Intenser all its odours rise,
As grief-worn spirits soften still
  Hard hearts with loving liquid eyes.
    Oh, more than rose, sweet blossom pale,
    I love thee, Lily of the Vale.

Beside the graceful golden broom,
  And sturdy, stubborn, daggered whin,
I first beheld thy arch of bloom,—
  Like virtue on the marge of sin;
So *one* with chaste retiring grace,
  I in the world's great tumult found,
In word and deed, in form and face,
  Meek loving kindness clothed her round.
    And thou to her love's message bore:
    Be thou love's herald evermore.

No prickly spears, or burning stings,
  My fondling hand or eyes repel:
Listen! and love triumphant rings
  From every tremulous silver bell.
Around thee hosts of glittering blades
  Sharp-pointed, broad, and burnished green—
Thou, lovely virgin of the glades,
  Art guarded, Nature's forest queen:
    Most modest gem of earth thou art,
    I'll wear thee ever near my heart.

The burning stars are letters bright,
  By which we spell the heavenly plan:
And humble flowers when read aright,
  God's goodness teach to wayward man:
Dear offspring of the bounteous earth,
  Fair children of the glorious sun,
Whether of high or lowly birth,
  I love you all—yet love I none
    Like thee, sweet blooming trembler frail,
    White timid Lily of the Vale.

1852.

THE CHEERY AULD MAID.

A GLENCAIRN LEGEND.

HAE laughed at the lasses, as aiblins ye ken,
An' jokingly rhymed them again an' again;
But now I'm repentant, the truth to be said—
The joy of all hames is a Cheery Auld Maid!

There are Jessies, an' Bessies, an' Kates by the score,
An' Marys, an' Nellies, an' Lizzies galore.
Wha, if they were absent our licht wad be gane,
An' many in darkness wad stumble alane.

One weel I remember,—but what's in a name,
Be sure in our land there are thousands the same,—
So gentle, so earnest, so kind and so dear,
A joy to the joyless—the cheerless to cheer.

The lads an' the lasses wad pour in her ears
The tale of their sorrows, their hopes, an' their fears:

Those aching heart swellings, sae painfu' to thole—
Our elderly maiden wad soothe an' console.

Judge not from her smile an' her brow sae serene
That her heart to excitement a stranger had been,
And never disturbed by the passionate throes
Of a love disappointed—the woe of all woes.

The gallant young sailor, the pride of her soul,
Volunteered, and set sail, for the perilous Pole,
Like many brave fellows for glory he yearned—
With cheers he departed, but never returned!

Three summers she watched by the *name* graven tree,
And silently gazed o'er the storm smitten sea.
When vanished all hope she devoted her days
To helping the helpless—the humble to raise.

One night in her shielan—forsaken, forlorn,
A lady found shelter—a baby was born:
The mither lies low in her grave by the Cairn;
ANNIE took to her bosom the mitherless bairn!

So carefully nursed, she grew graceful an' fair,
With eyes like the skies, an' like sunset her hair;
She won the leal heart o' the laird o' Kirkhall,
An' the mitherless bairn is the lady of all.

Her darling weel married, our maiden once more
Resumed her auld love for relieving the poor;
The sick and the simple, the halt an' the blind,
In the home of dear ANNIE some succour wad find.

THE CHEERY AULD MAID.

She moved through the vale like a soft summer
        breeze,
Bearing sweetest of perfume, all senses to please,
Like sunshine that blesses where'er it may fall,
Unconscious she gladdened the spirits of all.

When Katie, her sister, was drowned in the ford,
ANNIE took to her seat at the head o' the board;
Restoring some brichtness, assuaging all pain—
The young ones forgetting their mither was gane.

'Twas Auntie at morning, 'twas Auntie at nicht,
For Auntie alane could set a' matters richt:
To Auntie, kind Auntie, so close they wad cling;
For wha like dear Auntie sae sweetly could sing.

But Time's flying shuttle was weaving a pall;
Aunt ANNIE resignedly answered the call;
By the CAIRN in the GLEN she was solemnly laid,
An' Scotland lamented the CHEERY AULD MAID.

    1876.

A RAILWAY RHYME.

LONDON fever, fume, and fury,
    Restless, fretful, striving ever;
Never-ending crowds of people,
    Rushing, eddying, like a river;
Thanks to Science, by a mail-train
    Speeding swifter than the wind,
London hubbub, glare, and gaslight
    For a while I leave behind.

Through the dark I smell the clover,
    Dream of farms and days of yore,
When from mountains, streams, and woodlands,
    Rapture came, that comes no more!
Over bridges—over meadows—
    Onward dashing—hissing on!
Starry gleams from lowly casements,
    Tell of love in places lone.

With a shriek, a bound, a shiver,
    With a wild, unearthly scream,

Tunnelled, rumbling, rolling round us,
    Clouds of smoke and blinding steam.
Now arise the low of oxen,
    Now the bleat of lonely sheep,
Now the fluttering wings of wild birds,
    Startled from their silent sleep.

Valleys green and village brightness
    Quickly change to smoky towns;
There the ceaseless clang of hammers,
    There the grimy desert frowns.
Awful is at pitchy midnight,
    Mammon's church, with flaming spire—
Thirst of Plutus, what can slake it?
    Quenchless is its fierce desire!

Changed again!—the day is dawning:
    Grey and crimson fold on fold,
Soon, with blaze of glory round him,
    Rolls the Sun on car of gold.
Spirits doubtful fly before him;
    Deeds of darkness, hiding, rest:
All the earth in song adore him,
    Blessing ever, ever blest.

Now amid the moorlands dreary
    Winding, floats our vapoury trail:
Pant we on, yet never weary,
    Cleave the rock and leap the vale.
Far beyond shine grassy uplands:
    Dense the mist lies deep below;
Touching heaven are rugged hill-tops,
    Streaked with fire and capped with snow.

Here the husbandman is toiling;
　　Roses fringe his cottage door;
Children stretch and wave their bonnets—
　　Plenty crowns the threshing-floor.
Plenty, peace, and pure devotion,
　　Ever on thee, England, smile!
Thus I close each sweet emotion
　　Sketched 'twixt London and Carlisle.

1852.

MY LADY.

Y lady's young as well as fair,
　　Has sunny eyes and nut-brown
　　　　hair;
A smile from her would banish care,
　　So charming is my lady!

With her there is no vain pretence
Of sparkling wit,—but sober sense,
And modesty and innocence
　　Are cherished by my lady!

We met—I tell not where, or when,
My wooing words were few and plain;
She sweetly answered back again,
　　"I'm thine." God bless my lady.

Though age and care may deeply plough
Some furrows on her cheek and brow,
What she was first, she still is now,
　　My life, my love, my lady!

1854.

AUTUMN THOUGHTS.

THE leaves are falling! let them fall;
'Tis Heaven's supreme decree that all
    That lives must die:
A little while their glory shone,
A little more and they are gone,
    In death they lie.

Had we no death, what then were birth?
A cumberer of this pleasant earth,
    Where all is fair:
Through death alone is found the room
For budding hope, for mental bloom,
    And manhood rare.

Deny us death—destroy the chance
Of soul mature, the proud advance
    Of intellect;
Controlling, conquering every plan
That mars the onward march of man
    To high respect.

Where men, like granite columns, stand,
Obstructive of the good and grand—
    O welcome death!

They boast they change not! while they speak,
Their hearts are stayed: their power how weak—
    How false their faith!

The bar once broken—soon the tide
Of new opinion, deep and wide,
    Resistless flows:
As age must yield to eager youth,
So falsehood flies before the truth,
    And wisdom grows.

Man, proud of life! while living, heed
The myriad lives that die to feed
    Thy mortal part;
And when the immortal soul takes wing,
Those myriad forms again will spring
    From brain and heart.

The life which earth and air bestows,
Builds up the fabric of the rose:
    Then, earth to earth!
The flower, matured, gives up its seed;
The leaves dissolve—dissolving, feed
    A second birth.

The husk of flesh, the shell of clay,
Must to th' imperial soul give way,
    And let it fly—
Emancipated chrysalis—
From coils of pain, to boundless bliss—
    To never die!

What we call death, is only change
Of life, permitting souls to range
    Unfettered, free,

Through all the regions God has made,
In glorious sun or sombre shade,
    Eternally.

Thou body, brace thyself for strife!
Thou soul, prepare thyself for life!
    And whatsoe'er
Thy noblest nature feels is right,
For that unblenching, boldly fight;
    For God is there.

1852.

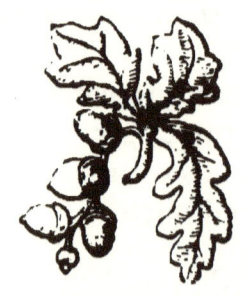

HORS DE COMBAT.

FLING open the windows wide for me,
   And let in the sweet, fresh air
That blows from the West so full
    and free,
   And over the heath so bare:
It comes with a message of health and rest,
From a beautiful home in the far-off West!

Oh! list to the voice of the cagèd lark,
  With carol so clear and loud,
Forgetting its freedom in grange and park,
   Its joy on the downy cloud!
    Imprisoned its wing, its spirit is free,
    And sweet is the lesson it brings to me!

My many companions have fled with glee
   Some up to the glaciers high,
Some on the moors, some on the sea,
   And some by the winding Wye!
    Whilst idly here I must lie and dream
    Of the restless rushing of life's great stream.

'Tis weary and hard for the active brain
  To be tethered to one small room;
A spirit all life to ever remain
  Benumbed by the lack of bloom,
    That comes when the body and spirit as one
    United can revel in shade and sun!

But pity me not, as I here recline
  Becushioned and couched with care;
In this feeble frame burns a fire divine,
  Which the shadow of grim despair
    Can never eclipse—for acutest pain
    My quenchless spirit revives again!

Keep open the windows wide for me,
  And let in the morning air
That blows from the west, from the cool salt sea,
  And over our heath so fair;
    It comes like a message of health and rest,
    From a dear, dear home in the far, far West!

1875.

OUR POLLY.

E knew not the love we had
          cherished so long
    As the light of our life and the
          life of our song:
    The star of our night and the sun
of our day
Are cloudy and dim since our Polly's away!

Till the last moment came and we found we must
    part,
'We knew not the cords she had twined round the
    heart:
Love grew with her growth, and we hoped she
    would stay—
Life has lost half its rapture now Polly's away!

So artless and guileless, so joyous and true—
A rosebud in beauty, and sweet as its dew:
So wise and so gentle—a lambkin in play—
Our summer's like winter now Polly's away!

Who now in the morning the posy will bring?
Or who in the evening delighted will spring

To meet us, and greet us, with laughter so gay?
Our nights have grown longer since Polly's away.

But girlhood will grow into womanhood soon!
Her lovely young dawn become beautiful noon;
May bright angels keep her where'er she may stray
In the land of the stranger—dear Polly's away!

Old feelings will deaden, new friendships arise
And cluster around her 'neath warm sunny skies:
Though she may forget us—old, wrinkled, and grey!
Her spirit will haunt us, though she's far away!

1869.

MY LOVE.

MY love is fair, my love is rare,
    And, oh! my love is kind;
Her heart's the throne of gentleness,
    And Heaven illumes her mind.
A halo round her forehead shines,
    Dissolving dark despair;
Beneath the sun there is not one
    In beauty half so fair.

Whene'er with maiden bashfulness,
    She turns her eyes on me;
Oh then they seem like mirrored stars
    When trembling in the sea.
With looks so kind they ever beam,
    Dissolving dark despair;
Beneath the sun there is not one
    In beauty half so fair.

When first I listened to the strain
    That from her sweet lips fell,

It chained in love my every sense,
And bound me like a spell;
A stream of richest music came,
Dissolving dark despair;
Beneath the sun there is not one
In beauty half so fair.

COME, COME, COME!

A SONG.

COME, come, come!
You know where the lindens bloom?
Come, come, come!
And drink of their sweet perfume:
Come, meet me, beloved, beneath their shade,
When day into night begins to fade.
A time for wooers and wooing made,
Is the twilight's deepening gloom:
Come, come, come!
My sweetest one, come, come!

Wait, wait, wait!
I will come unto thee betimes;
Wait, wait, wait!
I will come with the evening chimes;
I will come when shimmering up the sky
The wavering light retreats on high,
And darkening shadows inveiling lie
Beneath the odorous limes!
Wait, wait, wait!
Beloved one, wait, wait!

Here, here, here!
My beautiful met at last:
Here, here, here!
My sheltering arm thou hast;
The storms of life may fiercely blow,
And sorrow in surging tides may flow,
Whatever may come! come joy, come woe!
Thy refuge is in my breast,
Here, here, here!
Thy refuge for ever is here!

1875.

GOOD MORROW.[1]

GOOD morrow, good morrow! warm, rosy, and bright
Glow the clouds in the east, laughing heralds of light,
Whilst still as the glorious colours decay,
Full gushes of music seem tracking their way;
Hark! Hark!
Is it the sheepbell among the ling,
Or the early milkmaid carolling?
Hark! Hark!
Or is it the lark,

---

[1] One of the stanzas of this song was composed by the late Mary Russell Mitford, and appeared in her story of "Atherton." The other was written by Mr. Bennoch, at the urgent request of his much loved friend, M. R. M.

As he bids the sun good morrow?
      Good morrow;
Though every day brings sorrow!

The daylight is dying, the night drawing near,
The workers are silent, yet ringing and clear
From the leafiest tree in the shady bowers
Comes melody falling in silvery showers!
      Hark! Hark!
Is it the musical chimes on the hill,
That sweetly ringeth when all is still?
      Hark! Hark!
      O sweeter than lark
Is the nightingale's song of sorrow,
      Of sorrow;
Though pleasure will come to morrow.

1853.

MARY MILLIGAN.

MY bonny Mary Milligan,
   Twal dreary years hae gane
   Sin' we twa younkers through the
      woods
    Were wandering alane;
Were wandering alane in loe,
   As blythe as blythe could be;
I saw nae lass I loed but ane,
   An', Mary, it was ye.

Your hair was like the raven sheen,
   Like brichtest star your e'e,
And white as newly-drifted snaw
   Your bosom seemed to me;
Your voice was like the music made
   By birdies on the tree,
Sae cheerie, Mary Milligan,
   Were a' your words to me.

O bonny Mary Milligan,
   Ye'd lay your loof in mine,
An' I wi' loe an' innocence
   Wad press your fingers fine!

When on my breast your bonny brow
  To rest a wee ye'd lean,
Wi' very joy our hearts wad melt,
  An' tears fill baith our e'en.

There we wad sit in ecstasy,
  But ne'er a word we spak';
An' O the ties that Nature bound
  She surely winna break;
Time, Space, and Memory only make
  Ye through the distance seem
In beauty, like the heavenly things
  We whiles see in a dream.

But Fortune's ever-shifting wheel
  Has changefu' been to me,
And, bonny Mary Milligan,
  Has turned me far frae ye;
Has turned me far awa, my luve,
  Across the foamy sea;
But, bonny Mary Milligan,
  My heart's at hame wi' ye!

COME! GENTLE SPIRIT OF THE SPRING.

COME! gentle spirit of the Spring,
    Thou ever pleasant comer!
O quickly come, and with thee bring
    A foretaste of the Summer:
I long to climb the dewy wold,
    To feel the breezes blowing,
And watch the little flowers unfold
    Where yesterday 'twas snowing.

Through all the weary Winter time
    I could not but remember
The sudden squall that struck me down
    In dreary chill November,
O come and melt the icy care
    That fills my heart with anguish,
Breathe o'er me spring's delicious air,
    The air for which I languish!

Along the thymy sloping hills,
    The flocks are wending lea-ward;
Adown the glens the babbling rills,
    Are leaping gaily sea-ward;

136 COME! GENTLE SPIRIT OF SPRING.

The happy birds high overhead
   Are singing loud and mellow,
And earth awakening 'gins to spread
   Her blossoms white and yellow.

Far in the distance ocean wide
   Beneath the sun is glancing,
While through my brain a living tide
   Of joyous thought is dancing!
O now I feel the joy I sought!
   That ever pleasant comer
Has come at my behest and brought
   A foretaste of the Summer.

1858.

SPRING.

H! welcome Spring—delightful
    Spring!
  Thy joys are all begun,
Earth's frozen chain is rent in twain
  By heaven's reviving sun;
The dews of eve on meadows green,
  And waving blades of corn,
Like diamonds set on emeralds sheen,
  Are twinkling in the morn.
          Sweet Spring!

In thee the snowdrop finds a grave,
  Meanwhile the primrose pale
Grows meekly on the sunny bank,
  The daisy in the vale
With golden eye looks beautiful:
  Young trees fresh odours fling,
Their incense rises to the skies,
  In worshipping the Spring.
          Sweet Spring!

All living things that life enjoy
  Are now instinct with love;
In pairs fond creatures woo on earth,
  In pairs they woo above;

The echoing woods in music speak,
  When wingèd minstrels sing;
Uniting earth and heaven with song,
  In welcoming the Spring.
                    Sweet Spring!

Spring, Summer, Autumn, Winter,—all
  Their lessons read to man,
And teach him sorrow's not the end
  Of Heaven's benignant plan:
However great his cares may be,
  However deep their sting;
Like wintry winds they pass away,
  And welcome glorious Spring.
                    Sweet Spring!

MAY.

SWEET fragrance fills the dewy air,—
   Come, dearest, come away,
And in its rapture drown our care,
   For this is merry May!
    The merry month—the merry month—
The joyous month of May!
        Kind Nature brings
        Her sweetest things
To welcome merry May!

Glad music flows from hill and tree,
   Birds carol in the air,
And pour a stream of melody,
   To charm us everywhere.
Oh, the month—the merry month—
   The tuneful month of May!
        From woods and plains
        Rise cheerful strains
To greet thee Queen of May!

The joyous lambs around their dams
   Are bounding in their play:
Shall we be sad, nor seem as glad,
   Dear Margaret, as they?

In this sweet month—this dearest month—
  This cheering month of May—
      Shall we alone,
        'Neath heaven's bright zone,
Be sorrowful in May?

But fairest things at last must fade,
  And mould'ring pass away;
And so must we;—yet love shall be
  To us an endless May.
Oh, the month—the merry month—
  The charming month of May!
      True love shall be
      To thee and me,
A long, unchanging May!

1838.

A SPRING SONG.

SPRING-TIME returning sprinkles flowers
   O'er valleys, meads, and mountains;
The genial sun and gentle showers
   Unlock sweet Nature's fountains.
On joyous wing the wild birds sing
  With loud melodious voice—
"Oh, lovely Spring! thy blossoms bring,
  And bid the world rejoice."
    Spring-time returning sprinkles flowers
      O'er valleys, meads, and mountains;
    The genial sun and gentle showers
      Unlock sweet Nature's fountains.

In stream and lake, in wood and brake,
  All things that torpid lie
To life are stirred whene'er is heard
  Spring's carol in the sky.
When air and earth are full of mirth,
  Let each his tribute bring;
With loving heart bid grief depart,
  That all may welcome Spring.

Spring-time has come, and scattered flowers,
   O'er forests, meads, and mountains;
Hope joyous gilds the laughing hours,
   And music fills the fountains.

1855.

MARIAN.

A SONG.

BLOOM, bloom, beautiful flowers,
   And fling your scent on the wavy air;
Bear it, ye winds, to Marian's bowers,
   And tell her my spirit in love is there;
Tell her of honour and faith excelling,
   Tell her that love is the light of life,
The cloudly shadows of grief dispelling;
   And win—Oh win her to be my wife.

Fall, fall, perishing flowers!
   Odour, and beauty, and life are gone:
When leaves were falling in silent showers,
   Then Marian fell, and I am alone:
The gloomiest night still brings a morrow
   Of hope, to banish our fear away:—
My hour of peril, my night of sorrow
   Was beautiful Marian's dawning day.

1852.

A HISTORY.

I MET her first in early Spring,
A wild and wayward playful thing;
As here and there she flitting flew,
And left her footprints in the dew.
I marked her way from place to place,
As one a bounding fawn might trace.
A wilful, fitful, laughing thing,—
The joyous spirit of the Spring.

Through Summer days I followed still,
By singing stream and breezy hill;
Where nestling wild flowers sweetest grew,
Or softest breathing zephyrs blew;
Or gazing long on sea and sky,
Her soul sat glistening in her eye.
Thought's temple was her radiant brow—
She seemed the Summer's spirit vow!

When purple clusters bent the vine,
As one we walked, for she was mine!
Ah, me! I cannot, dare not tell,
How she with Autumn's fruitage fell;

I only know, with mournful face
Her shadowy form of love I trace;
And kneeling bend above the snow,
Where all I ever loved lies low!

1856.

TO THE HILLS AWAY.

WILL you come to my mountain
  home, love?
    Will you come to the hills with
      me?
    Through the wild woods we will
      roam, love,
  With our spirits light and free.
As free as the wind we will bound along,
  Your voice shall our music be;
Its love shall rival the bird's sweet song
  In its tuneful melody.
I'll deck your hair with roses rare,
  That grow on the gentle hills;
And weave a spell at the fairies' well,
  The source of the glancing rills.
Hark! hark to the woods, they shout Rejoice!
  Will you come love,—come to-day?
List! list to the sound of the wooing voice,
  To the hills! to the hills away!

To your mountain home I will go, love,
  I will go to the hills with you;
Through valley and wood we'll roam, love,
  When meadows are bright with dew.

TO THE HILLS AWAY.

O sweet is the song of the soaring lark—
 The linnet upon the tree;
But sweeter than birds are whispered words,
 That wooingly welcome me.
No roses rare shall deck my hair,
 As we gaily climb the hills;
The buffeting breeze that sways the trees,
 My spirit with rapture fills.
Then hie from the town to the breezy down,
 Nor loitering longer stay;
From the clear blue sky there cometh a cry,
 To the hills! to the hills away!

The whole of the first verse, with the exception of lines 11 and 12, is old, and said to be American.

1855.

SONG FOR THE SEASON.

JULY.

COME when the dawn of the morning is breaking,
  Gold on the mountain tops—mist in the plain;
  Come, when the clamorous birds are awaking
Man unto duty and pleasure again;
    Bright let your spirits be,
    Breathing sweet liberty,
Drinking the rapture that gladdens the brain.

High o'er the swelling hills shepherds are climbing,
  Down in the meadows the mowers are seen;
Haymakers singing,—and village bells chiming,
  Lasses and lads lightly trip o'er the green;
    Toying and wooing,
    Flying, pursuing,
Nature is now as she ever has been.

Then, when the toils of the day are all over,
  Gathered, delighted, set round in a ring;

Youth with its mirthfulness, age with its cheerfulness,
　Brimful of happiness, cheerily sing—
　　　"Bright may our spirits be,
　　　　Happy and ever free,
Blest are the joys that from innocence spring."

1852.

SONG.

THE setting sun throws o'er the sea
　　A glorious golden chain,
　Uniting lands in bonds of love,
　　To war no more again:
　　　Or is't a cheering smile from Heaven
　Borne o'er the glowing tide,
To bless two fondly-loving hearts
　Now beating side by side?

I am a child of Scotland's wild
　And rugged mountains blue:
Of England's wide and fertile plains,
　The fairest child are you.
By Heaven's example thus we join
　In love our father-lands;
No friend is he to thee or me
　Who'd burst the holy bands.

But what are country, friends, or home,
　Since, wheresoe'er we move,
Our two fond hearts will there create
　A world of joyous love?

Thy beaming eye shall be its light,
   Thy voice its melody;
Thy breath, more sweet than new-mown hay,
   Its atmosphere shall be.

REFLECTIONS.

WRITTEN AT GAINFORD SPA.

HOW calm—how still my spirit feels
   Within this quiet wood,
Where scarce a hum or passing
     breeze
   Awakes the solitude!

This footpath winding down the bank,
   That health-restoring spring,
These overhanging leafy trees,
   Sad thoughts upon me bring.

Each bough's the home of many a sigh,
   Each flower of many a tear:
When absent from the longing eye,
   My thoughts will wander here.

Who knows?—perchance our thoughts have met
   In this delightful scene,
Though parted, and ten thousand miles
   Of ocean roll between.

REFLECTIONS.

Where art thou now, my brother?—where?
    The echoing woods repeat;
Far o'er the sea thy lonely grave
    Is trod by strangers' feet.

Upon this elm, a sapling then,
    But now a stately tree,
Thy name was carved;—where is it now?
    No trace of it I see.

Grave lesson here for all who woo
    Ambition, power, or fame;
The name had long outlived the man—
    The tree outlives the name!

1840.

O, WHAT ARE YOU DOING?

 WHAT are you doing, sweet Nelly? says I:
O what are you doing, sweet Nelly, so sly?
It's this you are doing.
Some mischief you're brewing
You'll some day be ruing,
And blaming the beam of a certain black eye.

It's little in truth that I'm doing, says she;
O nothing at all I am doing—for he
　　Who promised to meet me
　　I'm thinking will cheat me—
　　'Tis cruel to treat me
So badly, and leave me alone as you see.

Just take my advice, little Nelly, says I:
O take my advice, and to follow it try.
　　You promised to marry
　　That do-nothing Harry!
　　But why should you tarry
For him any longer? let me be the boy!

[*Casts off disguise.*]

O how could you tease me so, Harry? said she,
When I'm dying to please you, my Harry McGhie.
    To come so disguised,
    Where true love is prized;
    But I'll do as advised,
And at Easter, dear Harry, we wedded shall be.

1856.

WHAT IS IT?

I.

WHAT is it? What is it? the little child said,
    As he played on the earthen floor,
With the patches of light which the sun had laid
    Through the chinks of a shattered door.
    They are shreds of white
    From the garments bright
Of the radiant sun on high.
Each mote in the beam has a silver ring:
Oh! silently listen and hear them sing.
As they eddying dance and fly!
    How high?
To their homes far up the sky!

II.

What is it? What is it? the young man said,
    On his cheek was a flush like shame,

While, dazzling shone from their dusky shade
  Two perilous globes of flame!—
      Of beaming eyes
      Askant—and sighs,
  Beware young man, beware.
They may bear you high, they may sink you low;
There is danger whithersoever you go:
  Of conscience alone take care!
      For there
  Is the peace that defies despair.

III.

What is it? What is it? the miser said,
  As he stammered, and clutched, and stared;
The gold he had gathered began to fade,
  Though only for gold he cared.
      In hoarding wealth,
      He had bartered health
And honour, and dwarfed his powers;
For self alone he had planted seeds,
For self he had reaped and garnered weeds!
  Mistaking the weeds for flowers:
      And cowers
From the blackness that over him lowers!

IV.

What is it? What is it? is always said
  Alike by the young and the old:
By their brightest visions they are betrayed,
  For they fade like a story told.
      Beneath the sun,
      Oh every one
  Some sickening sorrow hath.

Corroding, cankering day by day,
Flinging dark shadows across his way,
And they point—to the gulf of death,
Which saith,
Love honour, and die in faith!

1856.

MY OWN.

Y own! my own—all, all my own!
What rapture roused my childhood's joy!
That all to me, to me alone,
Should now belong that lovely toy!

As years flew by, and blood grew warm,
And deeper thoughts the heart employ;
One form alone had power to charm
The passion of the wayward boy.

But later still, when early thought
Had into flower and fruitage grown,
I clasped the being love had brought,
Rejoicing she was all my own.

And now, when spring and summer heat
Have into sober autumn blown,
I ever find my joy complete
In her who's evermore my own.

1875.

MASONIC SONG.[1]

WHAT is that I hear?
    Gently, faintly, knocking?
Some one claims our cheer:
    Hark! the echo mocking.
Masons all are kin:
Joyous we're together:
Bring the stranger in—
    And greet him like a Brother.
    Clink your glasses, clink:
        Set their lips a-ringing.
    Clink your glasses, clink—
        All in chorus singing,
Hurrah, hurrah, hurrah!
    What men may do, we dare, man:
Our guide, our life, our law,
    The compass, book, and square, man.

Just, upright, we stand—
    All that's false rejecting:
Loyal heart and hand—
    All that's good protecting.

---

[1] Originally written for the Lodge of St. John, No. 252, Thornhill, Dumfries-shire; but subsequently revised so as to make it acceptable to all other Lodges.

Knowledge keeps us free;
  Truth defends from danger.
Brethren! pledged are we
  To help the needy stranger.
    Clink your glasses, clink;
      Set their lips a-ringing.
    Clink your glasses, clink—
      All in chorus singing.
    Hurrah, hurrah, hurrah!
      The needy are our care, man;
    Our guide, our life, our law.
      The compass, book, and square, man.

When our work is o'er,
  Sweet is rest from labour:
Still there's work in store—
  Work to help a neighbour—
Work to heal the smart
  Of bitter grief and sorrow:
Cheer a Brother's heart,
  And make him glad to-morrow.
    Clink your glasses, clink;
      Set their lips a-ringing.
    Clink your glasses, clink—
      All in chorus singing,
    Hurrah, hurrah, hurrah!
      To help a friend, prepare, man;
    Our guide, our life, our law,
      The compass, book, and square man.

Fill again! and toast,
  Joy of every true man,
What we love the most—
  Woman—Sister! Woman!

Rosy, ripe, and rare,
　Lips with honey laden;
All that's good and fair,
　Whether Wife or Maiden.
　　　Clink your glasses, clink:
　　　　Set their lips a-ringing.
　　　Clink your glasses, clink—
　　　　All in chorus singing.
　　　Hurrah, hurrah, hurrah!
　　　　Our hearts with them we share, man,
　　　In honour, love, and law,
　　　　By compass, book, and square, man.

Brothers! when we part,
　Still remember duty:
Faithful hand and heart,
　True to love and beauty.
On the Square we stand—
　All that's bright before us—
Joyous! hand in hand—
　And Heaven smiling o'er us.
　　　Clink your glasses, clink—
　　　　Set their lips a-ringing.
　　　Clink your glasses, clink—
　　　　All in chorus singing.
　　　Hurrah, hurrah, hurrah!
　　　　Fraternity we swear, man:
　　　Our guide, our life, and law,
　　　　The compass, book, and square, man.

LOVE AND MARRIAGE. IN FIVE STANZAS.

I.—DESCRIPTIVE.

HOW pleasant to gaze where affection looks,—
Where palms are lessons, and eyes are books;
Where'er lovers wander, in sun or in shade,
Two kindred souls have an Eden made.
Amid olive groves by the tideless sea
They plighted their troth, and how happy was he;
I watched them long, and I see them now,
Supremely blessed in their hearts I trow.

II.—IMAGINATIVE.

Oh sweet are the greetings old friends renew,
As in parted clouds is a glimpse of blue;
How dear are the blossoms fond eyes discern
That nestle and smile 'neath an arch of fern;
And sweet is the music that wanderers hear
That tells of their distant homes so dear;
But sweeter than these—than all!—I prove,
Are hearts that in unison beat with love.

III.—SPECULATIVE.

Oh there is a maiden so fair to see,
I would she were willing to wed with me;
How happy were I if I could but rest
In the shade of the pansy that gems her breast;
Or she on my breast as mine repose,
Beside this blushing, love breathing rose.
The earth were heaven could I but feel
That she loved me, and called me her own Emile!

IV.—DECLARATIVE.

I looked like ice—though my heart was fire,—
And language declined to express desire:
I felt like a statue of dumb despair.
But somehow my feet ever wandered, where
I suddenly found, with glad surprise,
Love potently speaks through earnest eyes!
I silently wooed and won my bride,—
My beautiful Emma—my life, my pride!

V.—CONCLUSION.

Thus silently, suddenly, hastily won,
Two hands are united, two hearts are one.
Brush, canvas, and colours are cast aside
For cares and for duties becoming a bride.
She goes with our blessing—we all rejoice,—
Though some will be missing her cheery voice.
One star from the mountain has vanished away
To illumine the valley of lone Tenay.

LOVE'S CONSOLATION.

ENVY not the world its wealth,
    Nor mingle in its strife;
I'm happy in my lowly home,
    My children, and my wife:
Their cheering presence fills my heart
    With gladness day and night;
Approving smiles from those we love
    Make hardest labour light.

To feel a kiss from loving lips
    Imprinted on my brow,
Brings more of happiness, dear wife,
    Than princes ever know!
To hear our children laugh, and see
    Them playing on the floor:
O this, my dearest, makes us feel
    We never can be poor!

Our books are Nature's flowery vales,
    And heathery mountains high,—
The waving woods,—the foaming tides,—
    And Heaven's bespangled sky:

Our music is the song of birds,
    The humming of the bees,
The cadence of the murmuring streams,
    The sighing of the trees!

Our pilgrimage on earth, dear wife,
    Soon—very soon—may cease;
We're thankful still for many days
    Of bounteous love and peace:
Through life we have united been;
    And this I only pray:
One balmy gale at last may bear
    Our souls in bliss away!

DYING.

THE maiden raised her feeble form
  Upon the humble bed,
And, stretching forth her slender
    hand,
  In trembling accents said:—
"Dear mother, I am very faint,
  Some drink I pray thee bring;
And what will cool this burning pain
  Like water from the spring?

"Oh this is sweet!—'tis very sweet!
  I fain would drink again;
I feel it trickling here, and here,
  All through my heart and brain!
Now, mother, bring me gayest flowers,
  And leaflets young and green;
I'll make my love the fairest crown
  That poet e'er has seen.

"I'll bind it with my silken hair,
  And, mother, it will be,
When placed upon his lofty brow,
  Most beautiful to see!

My lips shall every leaf embalm,
    The humblest shall not fade;
My tears annealed, like living stars,
    Shall sparkle on his head."

The mother heard, obeyed, and smiled,
    Delighted thus to find
That reason's holy light again
    Illumed her daughter's mind.
" 'Tis finished, mother!—Oh, my heart
    Feels glad,—I know not why!
Thou'lt tell how truly I have loved,
    Nor shrank when death was nigh!

" Thou'lt place this on his head, I know;
    'Twill inspiration bring:
How happy they who then will hear
    How mournfully he'll sing!
His looks—methinks I see them now—
    Fall tenderly on me:
His image fills my weary eyes—
    I nothing else can see!"

The beam of bright intelligence,—
    A pure celestial ray
Of heavenly light,—no longer shone,
    But, darkening, passed away:
The eye resumed its wonted glare,—
    All meaningless its gaze,
And cold, as when through icicles
    The glimmering moonlight plays!

A few short hours she silent sate,
  Then heaved a doleful sigh;
And, staring into vacancy
  With frenzy-burning eye,
Exclaimed, "Ah! what art thou, dread form?
  Hurl not thy dart at me!
Thou hast!—Ah me! my lover's song
  Brings immortality!"

MINNIE AN' ME.

THE spring time had come; we were sawing the corn:
  When Minnie—wee Minnie—my Minnie was born;
    She came when the sweet blossoms burst for the bee,
An' a sweet bud o' beauty was Minnie to me.

The harvest was ower, and yellow the leaf,
When Mary, my daughter, was smitten wi' grief,
O little thought I my dear Mary wad dee,
An' leave as a blessing, wee Minnie to me.

O guard her, ye angels, an' keep her as noo,
A glint o' warm sunshine—a clear drap o' dew,
An' sweet as the hinny blob fresh frae the bee—
She is aw thae, an' mair, is my Minnie to me.

Her hair's like the lang trailing tresses o' night,
Her face is the dawn o' day, rosy and bright;
Sae bashfu', sae thoughtfu', yet cheery an' free:
She just is a wonder, my Minnie to me.

Her smile is sae sweet, an' sae glancin' her een,
They bring back the face o' my ain bonny Jean;
Mair sweet than the linties, that sing on the tree,
Is the voice o' my Minnie when singing to me.

For mony lang years I'd been doiting alane,
When Minnie revealed the auld feelings again;
In the barn or the byre, on the hill or the lea,
My bonnie wee Minnie is seldom frae me.

Wherever she moves she lets slip a wee crumb,
To beasties or birdies, the helpless an' dumb,
How she feeds them, and leads them, it's bonny to see;
Oh! a lesson o' loving is Minnie to me.

Whenever she hears my slow step on the floor,
She stands wi' her han' on the sneck o' the door,
An' welcomes me ben wi' a face fu' o' glee,
O nane are sae happy as Minnie an' me.

She trots to the corner, an' sets me a chair,
She plays wi' my haffets, and kames down my hair;
Or keeks through my specs, as she sits on my knee;
Oh wer't na for Minnie, I think I wad dee.

But I'll no talk o' deeing; some work may be done,
Or daundering dreamily, bask in the sun;
Till Providence pleases my spirit to free,
Oh! nae power shall sever my Minnie an' me!

1869.

ADAM BROWN AND JEANIE KENNEDY.

A BALLAD.

ADAM BROWN and Jeanie Kennedy
    were born i' the same year;
She doun by the Carron burn—he up
    at Durrisdeer;
The weans they toddled han' in han'
    an' sae thegither grew,—
Till as manikin' an' wifekin they're known the
    valley through.

They cleekit arm in arm as aye they laughin' gaed
    to schuil,
And learnt the shorter carritch in the mill ayont
    Drumcruil:
In the simmer she for Adam pou'd the gowans
    frae the braes,
And in autumn, for his Jeanie, Adam gathered
    nuts and slaes.

When either o' the bonny bairns the neebors ever
    saw,
They kenned fu' weel the ither ane would no be
    far awa;

They aye were drawn thegither, but they didna
    dree the charm;
She was weak, an' he was strong, sae he guarded
    her frae harm.

He grew like ony sturdy aik in glory on the lea,
An' she was like the ivy clinging close as ye
    might see;
Frae 'neath his strong protecting arm she smiling
    read his face,
As in return she lent to him her beauty an' her
    grace.

Like sister and like brither, they wad sit on the
    same seat
Wi' clasping hans, an' cheek to cheek, and whiles
    their lips wad meet;
They never spak a word o' luve, for deep down in
    the heart
The truth was cherished that o' ane the ither was
    a part.

As she grew up to womanhood an' he to manhood,
    sae
The time had come when he awa to foreign lan's
    maun gae;
The afternoon was cloudy, and the night was
    driving weet,
Yet they parted as if feeling they wad in the
    mornin' meet.

When mornin' came wee Jeanie's een were red
    an' dewy blind,
And ever she was looking for what she could
    never find;

O sad was she an' restless, yet she blushet like
    the haw,
As she ask hersel' the question—"Why did Adam
    gang awa?"

The simmer it had faded into autumn weird, a'
    that
Had glided into winter; cauld an' lanely Jeanie
    sat,
She fain wad greet and find relief, but sweet tears
    never came;
Yet aye she silent sighing prayed for Adam t'
    come hame!

Lang letters first, then shorter; then for months
    nae tidings came:
Jeanie feared he might be ailing, yet she didna
    Adam blame:
Jealous tongues let loose a whisper, O how rapidly
    it spread,
That Adam to a lady high in Canada was
    wed!

Wee Jeanie, she grew unco pale, the bloom it left
    her cheek,
She pined like ony lily, but she nae reproach wad
    speak;
"O weel kens he, his happiness was aw my aim
    in life,
Gude angels pour your blessings baith on Adam
    an' his wife."

But, whisht! there is a clicking at the sneck upo'
    the door,
A stranger man—a manly man—is standing on
    the floor!
She looks at him—she flies to him—she falls upon
    his breast,
"O, Adam, this is happiness"—"My Jeanie, I am
    blest!"

1875.

THE AULD, AULD STORY—LASSES BEWARE.

SWEET is the strife, and pleasant
    the life
  Of lasses when spirited, young,
    an' bonny;
  For maidenly charms draw lovers
in swarms,
  Like bees to the blossoms intent on honey;
    For health it is good as ane's daily food,
    A rapturous time is young maidenhood.

But whatten a life—O whatten a strife,
  When cheeks are a waning an' mair than thirty!
For how to get out of ane's maidenhood
  Is a terrible trouble—it is—my certie!
    It canna be guid to get thin in the bluid,
    Bewrinkled, an' still in ane's maidenhood.

THE AULD, AULD STORY.

In our beautiful glen there are mony young men,
   A' stalwart an' strong as a man should be;
They say I look weel, yet, rarely a chiel
   Slips in at the gloamin' a wooing o' me.
     I'm sairly afraid my chances are dead,
     An' I'm fated to live an' to die an auld maid.

A mettlesome lad frae ayont Drumwhad,
   Where shimmering babbles a burnie bonnie,
He babblin' plied his suit, an' I tried
   To like him, but wairsh, O wairsh was Johnnie!
     In sooth I'm afraid my fortune's in shade,
     An' I' doomed to shiver an' wither a maid.

It was nice to be clippet around the waist,
   An' hae noticed the shape o' my dainty feet;
Sae blate was the lout—he wad never speak out,
   Yet, O his kisses were saft and sweet.
     When gane, I'm afraid I wished he had
       stayed:
     To be somebody's wife, I wad sink the auld
       maid.

Syne a minister man, frae ayont Straquhan'
   Cam' flecchin' an' preachin'; I answered in
      haste—
He micht do for the heathen,—but wadna for
     me—then
   His way of conversion was no to my taste.
     He sighed an' he prayed I'd be Mistress
       M'Faed;
     That micht hae been wiser than pining a maid.

A lawyer came neist on a hard-ridden beast—
  Post obits, an' actions, sustained or condoned,
Laws Roman an' Gothic, kirk laws and hypotheck!—
    Intervening—I tauld him his suit was postponed.
      He scowlingly said, wi' a jerk of his head,
      He was foolish to think of a scraggy auld maid!

A doctor then cam' they ca'd Simpering Tam,
  Wha's potions were ready for ilka condition;
Wi' havering prattle he talked o' his cattle,
  But I turned me away frae this son o' perdition.
    He began to upbraid—half relenting, I said,
    There is spunk in the doctor; and still I'm a maid.

Ae nicht in my dreaming, I heard a bairn screaming,
  I cuddled and kissed it sae mitherly fain;
But I suddenly woke, an' the spell it was broke.
  I was aw on my wearisome pillow alane.
    I am mickle afraid that all hoping will fade,
    That I'll live discontented and die an auld maid.

Kind Heaven prevent I should live to repent
  Refusing all chances o' wifehood sae happy!
I fear I may fauld a man wizened an' auld
    Instead o' a young ane sae cozie an' crappie.
      Gae fetch me a plaid, I'll ride on a raid
      Ere I grow, as I'm growing, a shrivelled auld maid.

Just then frae Glen Shinnel cam' Donald
    M'Kinnel,
  A weel-to-do body wi' haffets like snaw.
As I gaed to the well, I just thocht to mysel'
  The auld ane is better than nae man ava!
    It weel may be said my conceit has been laid,
    But I'll drop the reproach o' a cankered
        auld maid.

Now I am his ain, I can see very plain
  He is doatingly fain o' his forty-year wife.
But a word in your ear,—nae pickle o' gear
  Can brim up wi' pleasure ane's measure o' life!
    O marriage is guid—it gladdens the bluid;
    An' onything's better than maidenhood!

As I sit in the kirk, the young lasses may smirk
  An' think I'm gaen gyted—what's that to me?
While Donald is kind, to their joking I'm blind—
  They'll be glad of my luck gin they bide a wee!
    I noo understand how marriage is grand,
    An' a WIFE is the noblest name in the land!

1875.

COILA.

READ AT A MEETING HELD IN COMMEMORATION OF THE BIRTH OF BURNS.

GAIN,—again assembled here,
    Are men with hearts and souls sincere,
    And eyes whose lustre with a tear
        Is dimmed for him of Coila!
Yes! here again a chosen few
Shall pay the grateful homage due
To him, the gentle, kind, and true,
        Who sweetly sung in Coila!

A title sumph was not his lot:
His birth-place was the peasant's cot:
When men have dotard kings forgot,
        They'll think of him and Coila.
He knew no rules nor studied art
By which his lays might reach the heart;
Of Genius' self he seemed a part—
        A genius born in Coila!

And as for laws, he needed none;
His thoughts were laws,—ay, every one,—
And universal as the sun
  That softly beams in Coila;
And nations yet unborn shall raise
Their voices tuned to notes of praise
Of him whose thoughts were turned always
  On liberty and Coila!

But where are they who made him wink
At things that were, nor *dare to think*,
But WORK, and thus coercive sink
  The mighty mind of Coila?
Yes! where are they?—You may ask where.—
In deepest gloom, or wheresoe'er
Base souls are found, you'll find them there,
  But not with him of Coila!

If ye his fame in truth would see,
Go search among the brave—the free:
There mark the freest soul,—'tis he
  Who loves the bard of Coila!
When hearts enslaved for freedom glow,
They feel their wrongs, and strike the blow.
Are *free!*—Go, learn who taught them so!
  They'll shout,—a voice from Coila!

The wand'ring exile doomed to roam
O'er deserts wild,—o'er Ocean's foam,—
Far, far from friendship, love, and home,
  Is still consoled by Coila!
He thinks not on the arid plains,
Nor fever raging in his veins,
For crooning o'er old Scotia's strains,
  He deems himself in Coila!

When virgin bosoms pant with love,
And dream of bliss whene'er they rove
By winding stream or balmy grove,
    O! then they think of Coila.
With passion quivering through the brain
They strive to speak, but ah! how vain,
Till Burns with magic rends the chain—
For who could willing love explain,
    Like him, the bard of Coila?

Whene'er the social few unite
To spend in joy the festive night,
The wit and wisdom dazzling bright
    Are borrowed beams from Coila!
Whate'er his theme, the poet shone;
The lyre he struck was all his own;
'Tis broken now,—the Bard is gone,—
    And Genius weeps o'er Coila!

TO THE MEMORY OF BURNS.

READ AT A MEETING HELD IN COMMEMORATION OF THE POET'S BIRTH.

MMORTAL Bard,—immortal Burns,
    The Patriot and the Prince of Song,
When friends are met shall they forget
    The honours which to thee belong?
            Immortal Burns!

In every land where truth is known,
    The musings of thy mighty mind
In strains of melting love have flown
    To fraternize the human kind,
            Immortal Burns!

Thy lays have seared the tyrant's heart
    Like flaming bars of hottest steel,
But raised the poor to know their right,
    To think as men,—as men to feel.—
            Immortal Burns!

When light, and hope, and reason die,
    And darkness shrouds the face of day,

And all things fade,—O, only then
    Shall Scotland's Bard in fame decay,
                Immortal Burns

With reverent silence we will fill
    A cup whene'er this day returns,
And pledge the memory of the Bard,
    The Bard of Nature—Robert Burns,
                Immortal Burns!

NITH.

NITH! my dear romantic stream,
    Lang may your waters flow
    In clear and quiet loveliness,
        Without a tale of woe.
Lang may the mists that rise frae ye
    Fa' in refreshing showers,
And bring fresh verdure to your meads,
    Fresh fragrance to your flowers!

Your course is like the human life,
    Sae changingly ye rin;
Here creeping slowly through the vale,
    There rolling o'er a linn.
Yet as ye wander on your way,
    All nature smiles on ye;
Ten thousand voices chant your praise,
    Frae bank, frae bush, and tree!

How oft upon your flowery banks
    At gloamin' I hae strayed,
Wi' Mary, blushing, young, and fair,
    My ain, my gentle maid;
How oft beneath the trysting-tree
    Thegither we hae stood,
An' gazed upon the moon's bricht ray,
    Clear, flickering in your flood!

'Twas on your banks that first we met,—
    Soft, murmuring did ye flow;
'Twas there I stole the first fond kiss,
    'Twas there we sealed the vow:
Whilst with our lips our troth we pledged,
    Mair lovely did ye seem;
We felt ye smiled approvingly,
    Dear Nith, belovèd stream!

The flowers may fade upon your banks,
    The breckan on the brae,
But O! the love I hae for ye
    Shall never pass away:
Though age may wrinkle this smooth brow,
    And youth be like a dream,
Still, still my voice to Heaven shall rise
    For blessings on your stream!

THE BARD'S RETURN.

SAIL on, sail on, my merry bark,
　　Dance gaily o'er the sea,
And bring me to my mountain home,
　　"Auld Scotia," brave and free;
Oh, now I see her warlike hills,
　　I love her more and more;
With child-like joy I bless the sand
　　That shines upon her shore!

The cloud-nursed mountains beckon me,
　　The valleys smile below;
The gentle streams, rejoicing, seem
　　To greet me in their flow:
Some boast of sunny eastern climes,
　　Where light eternal glows;
Where all is sunshine, man of life
　　But half its pleasure knows.

Give me the land of light and shade,
　　Of mountain and of river,
Where feeding streams from healthy springs
　　Make meadows verdant ever;

Where Winter brings his roaring floods,
    The spring flowers ever new,—
The Autumn brown and shady woods,—
    The Summer sunshine too!

Where Freedom first her standard raised,
    Despotic banners wave;
The iron heel of Tyranny
    Is trampling o'er her grave:
Those sunny lands are bound in chains!
    But, Scotland, still in thee
Men brave the terrors of the blast,
    And, like it, they are free!

Here are the winding woodland paths
    Where oft I've tarried long,
Entranced with forest music sweet,
    Fair Nature's soothing song!
And *there* a gentle maiden lived,
    The first my soul to move;
Whose smiles first twined around my heart
    The cords of early love.

She plaited me a laurel crown,
    I decked her hair with flowers:
The light of heaven ne'er dawned upon
    A happier life than ours:
We thought of love, we spoke of love.
    Love's breath perfumed the air;
Love reigned in heaven,—Love ruled on earth;
    'Twas love,—love everywhere!

Spirit of Life! grant, when I die,
    Like feelings may be given;

Then gently bear my soul away
    Unto a higher heaven:
From youth till now I've happy been,
    And why not in decay?
The sun as sweetly smiles on eve
    As on the rising day!

NITH REVISITED.

FLOW on, flow on, belovèd stream,
    My dear, delightful river,
By castles grey and meadows green:
    Flow on in peace for ever.
In youth I wandered by thy side,
    The Tynron hills before me,
And now as bridegroom loves his bride,
    In spirit I adore thee.

I'm wedded to thy glens and holms,
    So wild, so full of beauty;
The past into the present glides,
    And blends with love and duty.
I hear the pulsing evening breeze
    Among the branches beating;
My heart, attuned to winds and trees,
    The cadence is repeating.

High up the sky in clouds I trace
    The day's departing glory,
While by my side a sunny face
    Reflects a sweeter story:

NITH REVISITED.

The story of a loving life,
   The passing hours renew it;
Nor joy, nor care, nor worldly strife,
   Can conquer or subdue it.

The cloven rocks make dismal dens,
   In which your waters darkle,
Emerging from their gloomy glens,
   Oh how you dash and sparkle!
So life must pass through clouds and tears,
   Few rays of hope surrounding;
As mists roll off the sky appears,
   With light and love abounding.

Dear stream, thou emblem of my days,
   Thou child of moss and mountain,
My heart to thee would be of praise
   A never failing fountain.
So flow for aye, belovèd stream!
   Dear Nith, delightful river,
By castles grey and meadows green
   Flow on in peace for ever.

    1866.

TYNRON GLEN—THE SHINNEL.

'VE sung of Nith, I've sung of Scaur,
    I've sung of Annan Water;
And now I sing of Shinnel stream,
    Of Tynron hills the daughter.

Whence, trickling from its oozy source
    'Mong heather, bent, and rushes,
It broadens as it glancing runs
    Beneath o'erhanging bushes.

By Bennan's bonny woods and hills,
    Where babbling burns meander;
Where lasses gather nuts and slaes,
    And wooers love to wander!

Down Tynron Glen by Tynron Kirk,
    Where bells are gaily ringing;
Past Capenoch nestling in its woods,
    Where birds are sweetly singing.

There fishers cast the treacherous fly,
    Confiding trouts deceiving;
And children dip amphibious feet
    In bliss beyond believing!

TYNRON GLEN.

The sun shines down from cloudless skies
   On mountain, rock, and meadow;
Whilst browsing beeves beneath the trees
   Luxuriate in the shadow.

The sparrows' twitterings from the eaves
   Blend with the cushats' cooing;
Whilst playful lambs on grassy braes
   Their gambols are pursuing.

I've tasted much of joy in life,
   And deeply drank of sorrow;
If e'er o'erwhelmed with care or strife,
   I will from nature borrow

A thrilling sense of bliss supreme,
   Among these lovely mountains:
Inhaling wealth of mental health
   Near Shinnel's pleasant fountains.

No clearer sky or greener earth
   Were found at the beginning,
When first creation had its birth,
   And stars were set a spinning.

Here stands the ever open door,
   Inviolate from danger;
Where lavish hearts and clasping hands
   A welcome give the stranger.

O new-found friends on Tynron braes,
   O dear, delightful river;
O fair young buds of womanhood,
   May joy be yours for ever!

   1875.

SONG

FOR THE WISE AND TRULY TEMPERATE.

SEND the brimming glasses round,
    Make the beaming bubbles flicker;
Men o' sense will ne'er confound
    The wight who *wisely* topes his liquor.
    Pile with logs of pine the hearth;
Set the kettle's steam a reeling,
Waken we the sounds of mirth;
    Banish every fearsome feeling!
Biting blasts with icy flail
    Hills and howes are fiercely beating;
Wildest winds shall not prevail
    To chill the ardour of our meeting:
    Send the brimming glasses round,
        Make the beaming bubbles flicker;
    Men o' sense will ne'er confound
        The wight who *wisely* topes his liquor!

Frae Corsoncon to Shinnel-Head
    The dark, terrific storm is wheeling;
Gathering drifts, the shepherd's dread,
    Where the flocks an' herds are bieling:

SONG.

Craven spirits dangers fear,
   Men, as men should bravely meet them;
He alone deserves our cheer
   Who dares oppose, defy, defeat them!
     Send the brimming glasses round,
       Make the beaming bubbles flicker;
     Men o' sense will ne'er confound
       The wight who *wisely* topes his liquor!

Trusty neighbours, here's my loof!
   Strike and fear na! mak it tingle!
Care let fly ayont the roof;
   Friendship bleezes like the ingle;
Neighbours should as neighbours be,
   Heart wi' heart sae knit thegither;
Unsuspecting,—aye protecting
   All that's dear to ane anither!
     Send the brimming glasses round,
       Make the beaming bubbles flicker;
     Men o' sense will ne'er confound
       The wight who *wisely* topes his liquor!

Close the winnock, bar the door;
   Keep without the tempest railing,
Whilst within we gladly pour,
   To loyalty and love unfailing!
Here's to him we trust the most;
   Here's to lasses bright an' blameless;
Here's to her, our joy, our toast!
   Her the beautiful!—but, NAMELESS!
     Send the brimming glasses round,
       Make the beaming bubbles flicker;
     Mortal man shall ne'er confound
       The wight who *wisely* topes his liquor!

1877.

THE BONNIE BANKS O' DEE.

I'VE wandered by the sunny banks
    Of winding Forth and flashing Tay,
And drunk the wondrous beauties in
    Of Clyde, and Tweed, and mountain Spey;
But still with love unchanged I turn,
    And think of friends, who o'er the sea
As pilgrims, to auld Scotia came,
    To learn the charms of Royal Dee.

Balmoral's towers and shady bowers
    Loch Muick's waters, deep and cold—
Great Ben-Mac-Dhui, lifting high
    Above the snow his crown of gold.
Though wildness reigned on moory plain,
    From Aberdeen to bleak Braemar;
With loving faith we feared nae skaith,
    For love was our abiding star.

Where now we sit, have princes sat,
    Enraptured with the whispering din
Of Corriemulzie's elfin glen,
    Or Dee's dark, foaming, whirling linn.

THE BONNIE BANKS O' DEE.

Among the pines as day declines
　'Tis sweet to loiter, loving, free,
Or underneath the siller birks
　That shimmer on the banks o' Dee.

Wild roses scented ilka brae,
　Red clover flamed along the lea,
Bright heath and broom shed sweet perfume,
　But sweeter far my friends to me
The breezy hills, the rushing rills
　Attuned to nature's minstrelsy—
By night or day, though far away,
　We still remember bonnie Dee.

　1872.

COURTSHIP.

AN ARGUMENT IN FAVOUR OF BASHFULNESS.

YESTRE'EN, on Cample's bonny flood,
    The summer moon was shining;
While, on a bank in Crichope wood,
    Twa lovers were reclining:
They spak' o' youth an' hoary age,
    O' time how swiftly fleeting;
Of everything, in sooth, but ane,—
    The reason for their meeting!

When Willie thocht his heart was firm,
    An' micht declare its feeling,
A ray frae Bessie's starry een
    Sent a' his senses reeling;
For aye when he essayed to speak,
    An' she prepared to hear him,
The thochts in crimson dyed his cheek,
    But words would no' come near him!

Till Nature, gentle mither, came
    In pity to assist him,
And whispered something he maun learn—
    Her lesson quickly blessed him!

His arm around the lassie's neck
  He flung, nor think she spurned it;
Syne kissed her ripe and rosy lip,—
  Some say, the maid returned it!

'Tis ever thus that Love is taught
  By his divinest teacher;
He silent adoration seeks,
  But shuns the prosy preacher.
Now read me right, ye gentle dames,
  Nor deem my lesson hollow:
The deepest river silent rins,
  The babbling brook is shallow!

THE FLOWER OF KEIR.

H what care I where Love was born;
   I know where oft he lingers
Till night's black curtain's drawn aside
   By morning's rosy fingers.
If ye would know, come follow me
   O'er mountain, moss, and river,
To where the Nith and Scaur agree
   To flow as one for ever.

Pass Kirk-o'-Keir and Clover leas—
   Through loanings red with roses,
But pause beside the spreading trees
   That Fanny's bower encloses.
There knitting in her shady grove
   Sits Fanny, singing gaily;
Unwitting of the chains of love
   She forges for us daily.

Like light that brings the blossom forth,
   And sets the corn a-growing,
Melts icy mountains in the north,
   And sets the stream a-flowing:

So Fanny's eyes, so bright and wise,
    Shed loving rays to cheer us,
Her absence leaves us wintry skies—
    'Tis summer when she's near us!

O, saw ye ever such a face
    To waken love and wonder;
A brow with such an arch of grace,
    And blue eyes shining under!
Her snaring smiles, sweet nature's wiles,
    Are equalled not by many;
Her look it charms, her love it warms;
    The 'Flower of Keir' is Fanny!

1854.

THE DOMINIE.

YON gaudy house, like weel-faur'd sin,
    Belangs to Jock the Dominie:
It's fair without, an' foul within,
    Just like himsel',—the Dominie!
Oh, saw ye ocht like Dominie,—
    The mean,—the miser Dominie?
On earth's braid green there's nocht so mean
    As lang-legg'd Jock the Dominie!

The rattans rinnin' through the house,
    Like shadows, pass the Dominie;
And e'en the wee bit modest mouse
    Is starvin' wi' the Dominie.
Oh, saw ye ocht like Dominie,—
    The lang an' lanky Dominie?
His pow's sae bare, there's no' a hair
    To biel the louse on Dominie!

By a' the powers an' saints above,
    What think ye's come to Dominie?
He's fa'en out owre his lugs in love
    Wi' Kirstie, has the Dominie!
Her een like stars, sae burnin' bricht,
    Hae set on fire the Dominie;

THE DOMINIE.

A spark fell on his withered heart.
   An' maist consumed the Dominie!

Oh, luve maks fools o' wisest men,
   But Nature made the Dominie:
I fear he'll ne'er be richt again,
   In sic a plight is Dominie!
Yet Jock's a man o' consequence,—
   The parish clerk is Dominie;
Ae day, instead o' the response,
   "O Kirstie!" sighed the Dominie.

He taught the lass her A, B, C,
   To read an' write, did Dominie;
An' muckle mair, some people say—
   A libel sure on Dominie!
Whene'er he by young Kirstie sat,
   How fidgin' fain was Dominie;
He licked his lips, as fain to kiss—
   O fie upon the Dominie!

Lang years had rowed,—some sax or eight,—
   O'er Kirstie and the Dominie;
An' when she could nae langer wait,
   She ca'd a coof the Dominie!
O bonny, bonny Kirstie, take
   Some pity on the Dominie;
'Gin ye forsake, he'll drown himsel',—
   An' wha wad mourn the Dominie?

Oh, wae's me on the Dominie,—
   The puir, forsaken Dominie,—
Sin' Kirstie's wi' a packman gane,
   An' jilted Jock the Dominie!

THE DOMINIE.

" Farewell to joy,—farewell to mirth,—
   Farewell to life," sighs Dominie ;
" The only pleasure now on earth
   Is tawing bairns," cries Dominie !

" For God's sake, mind the Dominie !
   A deevil's grown the Dominie !
I fear he'll hang himsel' ere lang "—
   Ye needna fear the Dominie !
Yet pity for the Dominie,—
   The puir demented Dominie ;
The warl' wide has nocht beside
   Sae lanely as the Dominie !

NATURAL PHILOSOPHY.

EY, my bonny wee lassie,
    Blythe and cheerie wee lassie,
    Will ye wed a cantie carle,
        Bonny, bonny wee lassie?

"I hae sheep an' I hae kye,
I hae wheat an' I hae rye,
An' heaps of siller lass forbye,
    That ye shall spen' wi' me, lassie!
      Hey, my bonnie wee lassie,
      Blythe and cheerie wee lassie,
      Will ye wed a cantie carle,
          Bonny, bonny wee lassie?

"Ye shall dress in damasks fine,
My gowd an' gear shall a' be thine,
And I to ye be ever kind,
    Say,—will ye marry me, lassie?
      Hey, my bonny wee lassie,
      Blythe and cheerie wee lassie,
      Ye *will* wed a cantie carle!—
          Smiling bonny wee lassie?"

"Gae hame, auld man, an' darn your hose,
Fill up your lanky sides wi' brose,
An' at the ingle warm your nose,
　　But come na courtin' me, carle.
　　　　O ye clavering auld carle,
　　　　Silly, clavering auld carle,
　　　　The hawk an' doo shall pair, I trow,
　　　　　　Before I pair wi' thee, carle!

"Your heart is cauld an' hard as stanes,
Ye hae nae marrow in your banes,
An' siller canna buy the brains
　　That pleasure gies to me, carle!
　　　　O ye tottering auld carle,
　　　　Silly, clavering auld carle,
　　　　The hound an' hare may seek ae lair,
　　　　　　But I'll no sleep wi' thee, carle!

"I winna share your gowd wi' ye,
Your withering heart an' watery e'e;
In death I'd sooner shrouded be,
　　Than wedded to ye, auld carle!
　　　　O ye tottering auld carle!
　　　　Silly, clavering auld carle,
　　　　When roses blaw on wreaths o' snaw!
　　　　　　Then I will bloom on thee, carle!

"Gae hame, auld man, an' darn your hose,
Fill up your lanky sides wi' brose,
An' at the ingle warm your nose,
　　But come na courtin' me, carle.
　　　　O ye clavering auld carle,
　　　　Silly, clavering auld carle,
　　　　The hawk an' doo will pair, I trow,
　　　　　　Before I pair wi' thee, carle!"

THE TOCHER.

"I HAE na for your dochter,
　　High titles, lan', or gear!
I hae na for your dochter,
　　A thousand pounds a year!
But I can share, 'gin she'll be mine.
　　A heart that's leal and true,
An honest pride o' honest worth,
　　That princes canna boo!
A head to think, and hands to work,
　　Are a' I promise ye:
And they shall work your dochter's weal
　　Until the hour I die."

"You're welcome to my dochter,
　　Sae bonny, young, and fair,
You're welcome to my dochter,
　　Oh cherish her wi' care;
And if she makes as gude a wife
　　As mine has done to me,
Your fortune ye will never rue,
　　But happy ever be;
For *duty* guides my dochter's heart,
　　Wi' joy to you I give her:
The *worthy* choice a dochter makes,
　　A parent shouldna sever."

THE SCOTTISH GATHERING.
1868.

WHERE'ER the Scots wander, auld
  Scotland is near them,
    Her glory to gladden—her story
      to cheer them,
    Though far frae the heather, they
gather thegither,
An' lovingly help a less fortunate brither!
    Sae, a health to the banner that's floating
      above us!
    A health to the lasses who tenderly love us!
    A health to auld Scotland—glen, mountain,
      an' heather!
    Here's to the tartan plaid, bonnet, an' feather!

The time has gane by when the clans o' the Hielans
Delighted in raids on the Lowlanders' shielans;
Nae strife is now found atween one an' the ither,
But striving wha maist can befrien' a puir brither.
    Sae, a health to the banner that's floating
      above us!
    A health to the lasses who tenderly love us!
    A health to auld Scotland—glen, mountain,
      an' heather!
    Here's to the tartan plaid, bonnet, an' feather!

Nae man is exempted frae trials an' crosses,
Nae man can escape frae life's troubles an' losses:
An' wha wad escape, when we gather thegither.
The duty o' helping a heart-stricken brither?
    Sae, a health to the banner that's floating
        above us!
    A health to the lasses that tenderly love us!
    A health to auld Scotland—glen, mountain,
        an' heather!
    Here's to the tartan plaid, bonnet, an' feather!

When sick or in sorrow, gae find them wi' nurses:
When poverty presses, out, out wi' your purses,
As quickly as erst ye were out wi' the claymore
Defending pure honour!—Oh! what can we say
  more?
    Then, a health to the banner that's floating
        above us!
    A health to the lasses who tenderly love us!
    A health to auld Scotland—glen, mountain,
        an' heather!
    Here's to the tartan plaid, bonnet, an' feather!

A health to the chief who is owre us presiding:[1]
May 'Truth, Love' an' Honour be wi' him abiding:
An' a' through his days 'twill be joy to remember,
His presence made simmer o' murky November.
    Sae, a health to the banner that's floating
        above him!
    A health to the lass wha may tenderly love
        him!
    A health to auld Scotland—glen, mountain,
        an' heather,
    Here's to the tartan plaid, bonnet an' feather!

---

[1] Marquis of Bute.

"I DINNA KEN WHAT IS THE MATTER AVA."

 DINNA ken what is the matter ava,
I canna tell what is the matter ava,
For somehow or other I've gotten a thraw,
O I canna think what is the matter ava!

" Ae nicht at the gloamin', when herding the kye,
The canty young laird o' Drumshinnoch came by;
He kissed me sae often, that ever sin syne
I'm sure that my senses hae never been mine!
    I dinna ken what is the matter ava,
    I canna tell what is the matter ava,
    For somehow or other I've gotten a thraw,
    O I canna think what is the matter ava!

" My father an' mother an' sisters an' a',
May kiss till they're tired, it's like naething ava:
But aye when the lips o' the laird gied a smack,
My heart it was louping as if it wad break!
    I dinna ken what is the matter ava,
    I canna tell what is the matter ava,
    For somehow or other I've gotten a thraw,
    O I canna think what is the matter ava!

"My roupit auld grannie says gi'ing a kiss
To a callan is wrang, but I ken it is bliss;
There's muckle o' pleasure but naething o' pain,—
Were he here at this moment I'd kiss him again!
    I dinna ken what is the matter ava,
    I canna tell what is the matter ava,
    For somehow or other I've gotten a thraw,
    O I canna think what is the matter ava!

"Wi' the kye i' the byre, or the sheep on the hill,
The laird like a shadow is haunting me still,
An' e'en on my pillow, as dreamin' I lie,
I think him aside me, I canna tell why!
    I dinna ken what is the matter ava,
    I canna tell what is the matter ava,
    For somehow or other I've gotten a thraw,
    O I canna think what is the matter ava!

"Yestre'en my douce mither an' I were alane,
I tauld her the story again an' again;
She laughingly answered, scarce able to stan',
'Ye clavering hissie, ye're wanting a man!'
    I dinna ken what is the matter ava,
    I canna tell what is the matter ava,
    For somehow or other I've gotten a thraw,
    O I canna think what is the matter ava!

"'Mind, lassie, whenever he's wantin' a kiss,
Your tongue maun say *no*, though your e'es
    looking *yes;*
'Gin ever he speaks about marriage ava,
Look down to the groun', wi' a sigh saying na!'
    I dinna ken what is the matter ava,
    I canna tell what is the matter ava,
    For somehow or other I've gotten a thraw,
    O I canna think what is the matter ava!

"'Remember, dear Jeanie, ye keep my advice;
He'll lo'e ye the mair for denying him twice;
But venture nae farther, I pray you tak' tent,
While hummin' an' ha'ing, be sure ye consent.'
  I dinna ken what is the matter ava,
  I canna tell what is the matter ava,
  For somehow or other I've gotten a thraw,
  O I canna think what is the matter ava!

"The high in the warl' may do as they choose,
My heart it is honest, I canna refuse;
Forgetting the sin o't, what gude can there be
Saying *no*, when ye ken ye are tellin' a lie!
  I dinna ken what is the matter ava,
  I canna tell what is the matter ava,
  For somehow or other I've gotten a thraw,
  O I canna think what is the matter ava!

"My mother may talk as she likes about 'No,'
Though the word were salvation I could na say so,
'Gin Willie e'er speaks about marriage again,
Our auld Parish Priest shall make Jeanie his ain!
  For noo I ken what is the matter an' a',
  For noo I ken what is the matter an' a',
  I want to get married to Willie that's a',
  And naething beside is the matter ava!"

"PRIDE MAUN LEARN TO FA'!"

THE lasses are surely gaen gyte,
    Sic maigrims come into their heads,
An' mak' them sae saucy an' proud
    They wunna e'en mak' their ain
        beds.
The mither rins but an' rins ben;
    The mither may muck the byre,
But, save us, the dochters sae fine
    Do naething but whinge by the fire!
        Och on! it's a desperate thing,
        I dree it will ruin us a',
        An' sorrow on ilka ane bring;
        But " Pride maun learn to fa'!"

There's Peggy and Jessy and Jean,
    An' clavering supple-backed Nell,
By flowering o' kirtles for leddies,
    They think they are leddies themsel';
Wi' feathers an' flounces an' fans,
    O wow! but they think they look braw,

And strut as despising the grun';
　But "Pride maun learn to fa'!"
　　　Och on! it's a desperate thing,
　　　　I dree it will ruin us a',
　　　An' sorrow on ilka ane bring;
　　　　But "Pride maun learn to fa'!"

If chancely a callan comes near,
　A lad o' their ain degree,
They geck up their heads wi' a sneer,
　"How daur ye be fashing wi' me?"
Unless he's a laird or a priest
　They winna look on him ava,
Or a doctor or lawyer at least:
　But "Pride maun learn to fa'!"
　　　Och on! it's a desperate thing,
　　　　I dree it will ruin us a',
　　　An' sorrow on ilka ane bring;
　　　　But "Pride maun learn to fa'!"

The time has been seen when a queen
　Wad step frae her throne, sae hie,
To wed wi' a lad she could loe,
　Though come o' a nither degree.
O sirs! how the warl' is changed,
　There's naething but *leddies* ava,
Sin' *women* they scorn to be ca'd;
　But "Pride maun learn to fa'!"
　　　Och on! it's a desperate thing,
　　　　I dree it will ruin us a',
　　　An' sorrow on ilka ane bring:
　　　　But "Pride maun learn to fa'!"

"PRIDE MAUN LEARN TO FA'!"

When roses hae fa'en frae the cheek,
  The lightnin' left the e'e,
And shins growin' skinny an' weak,
  I trow she will then stoop a wee,
For sooner than die an auld maid,
  Wha's comforts are, truly, but sma',
She'll e'en coup creels wi' a cadger—
  He's better than naething ava!
    Och on! it's an excellent thing,
      An' should be a lesson to a',
    That whether in cotter or king,
      " Pride—pride maun learn to fa'!"

MY JOHNNY.

HAE ye seen my auld gude man,
  O hae ye seen my Johnny?
It's heaven to a woman's e'e
  To look on sic as Johnny!

The daisies growin' on the lea,
  Sae modestly an' bonny,
How sweetly aye they smile on me,
  When I am wi' my Johnny!
In youth I buxom was an' braw,
  Had wealthy wooers mony;
For honest lo'e I turned frae a',
  An' buckled wi' my Johnny!
      O hae ye seen my auld gude man,
        O hae ye seen my Johnny?
      It's heaven to a woman's e'e
        To look on sic as Johnny!

Our bairns like blossoms round a tree
  Hae grown about us thriving,
'Twould glad your heart could ye but see
  How they for us are striving!
As hirpling down the hill o' life,
  What happiness it gies us,

MY JOHNNY.

To see our bairnies, young an' auld,
  Sae eydent strive to please us!
    O hae ye seen my auld gude man,
      O hae ye seen my Johnny?
    It's heaven to a woman's e'e
      To look on sic as Johnny!

O mony a joyous nicht an' day
  I've shared wi' my auld crony;
Come weal, come wae, O come what may—
  I'll ever bless my Johnny!
His look sae kind, sae clear his mind,
  His brow sae high an' bonny;
Auld Nature vows she has na power
  To mak' another Johnny!
    O hae ye seen my auld gude man,
      O hae ye seen my Johnny?
    His loe is life an' mair to me,
      My *life o' life* is Johnny!

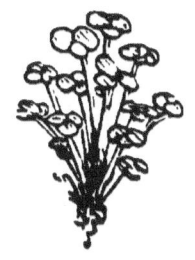

SONG.

OH, Jenny was bonny an' blythsome as ony,
   'Mang a' things o' nature the fairest was she;
      Her parents they flyted, because that she slighted
   The LAIRD wi' his fame an' his titles sae hie.

" Ye gawkie, what gars ye gae lo'e that bit callan,
   When ye, in your silks an' your satins sae braw,
As lady o' WROTHAM may ride in your carriage,
   Wi' gowd in your coffers an' wealth in your ha'?"

Thus spake her auld mither; and next came her father,
   In pride disappointed, oh, angry was he!
" The dochter wha weds 'gainst the will o' her sire
   On earth, e'en in *heaven* accursed shall be!"

" I lo'e ye, my father—I lo'e ye, my mither,
   My duty has ever been yours frae my birth;
But now it is Willie's.—if lo'eing him dearly
   Be sinning in HEAVEN, 'tis pleasant on earth.

" The laird may hae riches, an' title, an' splendour,
　　An' lands stretching out mony miles frae the sea;
But vain are his riches, and vainer his grandeur,
　　Compared wi' the kiss that my WILLIE can gie."

Oh, fathers and mithers, in right o' their station,
　　May preach an' beseech till the day that they dee;
But lo'e it will creep in when parents are sleeping,
　　An' bask in the beams o' a bonny bricht e'e.

The nicht it was dreary, the auld folks were weary
　　(But lo'e never doses, nor slumbers ava);
The lassie she fled to the arms o' her deary,
　　And now she is Willie's in spite o' them a'.

MY BAIRNIE.

FAIN wad lay me doun an' sleep
　　Where a' I love's reposing;
My wakefu' e'en sad vigils keep,
　　An' hunger for their closing:
I lo'e to hear the bird that sings
　　Where day by day I wander;
A wee han' tugs at my heart strings,
　　An' gently leads me yonder.

Near Kirk o' Keir we kept our tryst,
　　There Rob an' I were married,—
Oh waes me!—there my first, my last,
　　My wee, wee bairn I buried.
On that green grave I learn to dote,
　　It hauds my life's ae jewel;
Though I revere the han' that smote,
　　Oh, ance I though it cruel!

High up the lift the laverock soars
　　Like some kind spirit sent me,
To link my lowly hopes an' fears,
　　Wi' joys a wee while lent me.

When mournfu' winds awake the trees,
  I canna keep frae sighing;
A wee voice floats alang the breeze,
  Like soul to soul replying.

It is! it is! my bairnie's voice
  Sae sweet! but sad an' eerie;
For evermair it seems to say,
  "Come, mither! how I weary!"
Oh whisht, whisht, whisht, my wee, wee bairn!
  I feel, whate'er betide me,
Before the spring flowers bloom again
  I'll lay me down beside thee.

SONG.

H, life it is dreary,
    How dreary to me!
Of life I am weary
    When parted frae ye.
Then say the word, lassie,
    And banish my pain;
Come, answer me, Jessie,
    Will ye be my ain?

Death feeds on your silence,
    But why need I fear?
Sin' the voice in your smile,
    An' the tongue in your tear,
Are speakin' your feelings
    In language divine,—
"Be faithful, dear Robin,
    And Jessie is thine!"

"Thus on your bonny brow,
    Thus on your cheek,
I seal my devotion,
    For words are owre weak;
Through life wi' its changes,
    Dear Jessie, we'll prove
How blest are the beings
    United by love!"

THE PARTING.

FAREWEEL!—fareweel, an' we maun part
   May-be to meet nae mair:
The cords ye've bound around my heart,
   To rend I canna bear;
For wi' my life ye're sae entwined
   By nature's first decree,
That only ye o' womankind
   Can soothe or gladden me.

As licht is to the teeming earth,
   As sweetness to the bee,
As water to a parched tongue,
   Sae dearest ye're to me;
Your glancing e'en sae bonny blue
   Aye beam on me sae fair,
That shone the stars in heaven sae bricht,
   I'd aye be gazing there.

The miser lo'es his hoarded gear,
   The warrior lo'es his fame,
An' monarchs lo'e their proud estate,
   But what care I for them?

For wealth, nor fame, nor jewelled crown,
  Could pleasure bring to me,
Unless, sweet heart—my dearest part,
  They a' were shared wi' ye.

MARGARET.

THE moon is shining, Margaret,
  Serenely bright above,
And, like my dearest Margaret,
  Her every look is love!
The trees are waving, Margaret,
  And balmy is the air;
Where flowers are breathing, Margaret,
  Come, let us wander there!

The gentle river, Margaret,
  Is murmuring low and deep;
'Tis Nature's music, Margaret,
  Singing the world to sleep.
It's winding way, my Margaret,
  You ever love to see;
Come, come, my own dear Margaret,
  And wander there with me!

How proud am I, sweet Margaret,
  Thus wandering by thy side;
'Tis bliss to know, my Margaret,
  Thou soon wilt be my bride!
Yes! there's a hand, dear Margaret,
  A heart it gives to thee;
When Heaven is false, my Margaret,
  Then I will faithless be!

WILLIE.

WAE is me to part wi' ye !
    An' maun ye cross the sea, Willie?
Gin it be sae, then gang your way,
    An' Heaven smile on ye, Willie.
    Will ye think on me, Willie,
      As I think on ye, Willie ?
Baith nicht an' day, where'er ye gae,
    Your sister's heart's wi' ye, Willie !

Oh, swiftly sail the ship that bears
    Ye owre the foamy sea, Willie;
May balmy gales your life renew,
    An' waft ye hame to me, Willie !
    Think ! oh think on me, Willie,
      As I think on ye, Willie :
The joy, the bliss,—wha can express,
    When ye come hame to me, Willie !

If prayers can move the heart o' Love,
    And He in smiles look dune, Willie,
Though oceans wide our lives divide,
    We'll meet in bliss aboon, Willie.

Ye will think on me, Willie,
　　As I think on ye, Willie;
Baith nicht an' day, though far away,
　　Your sister's heart's wi' ye, Willie.

TO ISABEL.

H, were I as I ance hae been,
　　An' ye as ye are now,
I'd fainly fauld ye in my arms,
　　An' kiss your bonny brow!
　　I'd kiss your bricht and bonny brow.
An' drink life frae your een;
But, oh, this canna be, for now
　　I'm no' as I hae been!

Your life is like the living sun,
　　That gies life to the plain;
Though clouds awhile may dim his smile,
　　He'll brighter beam again.
I wouldna be the cloud that comes
　　Atween your love an' ye;
Your life's sweet light—the light o' lo'e,
　　Lo'e glentin' frae the e'e.

Wi' brother's lo'e I'll lo'e ye still,
　　Nor seek your heart to win;
For less to think, an' mair fulfil,
　　In me wad be a sin:

But there can be nae sin, sweet lass,
    In prayin', while awa',
That joys frae ye may never pass,
    But blessings on ye fa'!

THE DYING DAUGHTER.

H, I am unco laith to gang
    An' leave this warl' sae bonnie;
Oh, I am unco laith to gang
    An' leave this warl' sae bonnie:
It's no' because the warl's fair,
Has flowers to love, an' vocal air,
But 'tis to leave my frien's sae rare,—
    And you my faithfu' mither.

"Nae mair shall Willie need your care,
    For he has ta'en anither
To share his joys—his grief to share,—
    May they be blest thegither;
Poor Meggie's weary, worn an' weak—
Sad secret tears hae bleached her cheek,
My bitter fears I daur na' speak;
    Oh nurse her kindly, mither.

"Ye'll lay me down where Ellen sleeps—
    There softest winds are sighing:
For, O, I'd like that frien'ly feet
    Should linger where I'm lying;

I'll may be hear your gentle tread
As ye pass lightly o'er my head;
For, though I'm low amang the dead,
   I'll ken your footfa', mither.

"Now dinna weep—O, dinna grieve,
   My tender-hearted mither:
Nor sob sae deep—I only leave
   This warl' to find anither;
Yestreen I thrice heard Ellen say,
'Come, sister Lizzy, wherefore stay?'
Again she whispers, 'Come away!'"
The soul has fled, an' clay is clay—
   Despairing weeps her mither!

THE SHEPHERD'S PLAIDIE.

"DINNA fear, dinna fear,
    Dinna fear, my bonny lady;
Dinna fear, dinna fear,
    I'll shield thee in my shepherd's plaidie!
The howling winds may loudly blaw,
The arrowy sleet may fiercely fa',
My trusty plaid will turn them a',
    There's comfort in a shepherd's plaidie."

" Na, na, na!—Na, na, na!"
    Replied with haste the blushing lady;
"Na, na, na!—Na, na, na!
    I winna come within your plaidie.
I weel can thole the storm severe,
But not the wounded spirit's tear;
O smiling I can suffer here,
    But darena share your shepherd's plaidie."

"Dinna fear, dinna fear,
    Dinna fear, my bonny lady;
Dinna fear, dinna fear,
    True hearts are found beneath the plaidie."

The swelling storm in fury swept,
The trembling lass for shelter crept.
A marvel! she has never wept—
  A shepherd's wife, she loves the plaidie.

THE BONNIE BIRD.

H, where snared ye that bonnie, bonnie bird,
  Oh, where wiled ye that winsome fairy?
I fear me it was where nae truth was heard,
  And far frae the shrine o' the guid St. Mary?

I didna snare the bonnie, bonnie bird,
  Nor try ony wiles wi' the winsome fairy;
But won her young heart where the angels heard,
  In the bowery glen o' Invercary!

An' what want ye wi' sic a bonnie bird?
  I fear me its plumes ye will ruffle sairly;
Or bring it low down to the lane kirkyard,
  Where blossoms o' grace are planted early!

As life I love my bonnie, bonnie bird,
  Its plumage I never will ruffle sairly;
To the day o' doom I will keep my word,
  An' cherish my bonnie bird late an' early.

THE BONNIE BIRD.

Oh, whence rings out that merry, merry peal?
   The sang an' the laugh, they are chorused rarely;
It is!—it is the bonnie, bonnie bird,
   Wi' twa sma' voices a' piping early.

For, he didna snare the bonnie, bonnie bird,
   Nor did he beguile the winsome fairy;
He had made her his ain, where the angels heard,
   At the holy shrine o' the blest St. Mary.

SONG.[1]

O STAY WI' ME NOW, LASSIE.

STAY wi' me now, lassie, stay wi' me now;
O stay wi' me now, an' believe me;
   That this heart sae fain an' true,
   Shall be ever leal to you,
O dinna dinna think I'll deceive thee.

O how can you dare, laddie, how can you dare;
O how can you dare to come near me?
   When down in yonder glen,
   Lives the kindest o' auld men,
Wha has routh o' gear an' lan for to cheer me.

---

[1] One verse is old, by whom written I know not. The other two were written for a friend. The air is very beautiful.

O how can ye gang, lassie, how can ye gang.
O how can ye gang sae to grieve me?
    Wi' your beauty an' your art,
    Ye hae broken my heart,
O' I never never thought ye would leave me.

KATE.

H, bonnie wee Kate
  Sae blythe and blate,
When will she promise to be my mate:
  When will she come
  To gladden my home,
And make what is mine her ain, O?
Through bonny Dalveen
I gaed yestreen,—
My guiding stars were her glancing e'en;
  If waiting for me
  By the hawthorn tree,
    O why should I plead in vain, O?

Adown the gill,
Down by the mill,
Over the brow of the thorny hill,
  We wandered late,
  And I whispered, "Kate,
    How weary is life alane, O!

O Kate, be mine,
And a light divine,
Will ever along our pathway shine!"
    Her hand I pressed,
    And her lips confessed
        Next Summer she'd be my ain, O!

Nae birds in bowers,
Nae bees in flowers,
Ken half the pleasure that now is ours
    'Tis all delight
    From morn till night,
        And life has never a pain, O!
My joy, my pride,
My bonnie wee bride,
Is Katie, the flower o' Carron side;
    Words canna reveal
    The bliss I feel
        Sin Katie is all my ain, O!

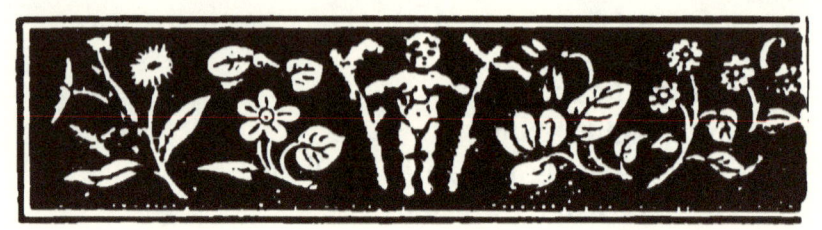

THE COVENANTERS.

A NITHSDALE BALLAD.

NITHSDALE men, your sinews brace,
    Sword and spear and gun have ready,
  Meet the King-hounds face to face,
    Eyes and ears alert and steady!
Dunscore—Closeburn—Tynron—Keir!
  Crichope, Scaur, and Carron Water!
Wild, heroic Durrisdeer!—
    To arms! to arms! prepare for slaughter.
  For the Faith our fathers fought,
    Martyred spirits will befriend us!
  Tyrants shall be brought to nought!
    "God of Liberty, defend us!"

Come from glen and craggy steep,
  Mountains green and hills of heather!
Sacred aye the watchword keep,
  Serried close, we'll march together!

See! they come adown the glen;
   Banners waving, bugles blowing!
Meet them, beat them, man to man—
   To all but Lag[1] our mercy showing.
     For the Faith our fathers fought
       Martyred spirits will befriend us!
     Tyrants shall be brought to nought
       "God of Liberty, defend us!"

Mark the onset; foot to foot,
   Plumed crest with bonnet blending,
Charge on charge, with shout on shout,
   Prayers and curses wild ascending!
Charge again! they waver—wheel!
   Hurrah! the Red Dragoons are flying.
Follow! Follow! God be praised—
   Tend we now the dead and dying;
     For the Faith our fathers fought
       Martyred spirits have befriended!
     Tyrant councils brought to nought!
       "God of Liberty defended!"

Out-manœuvred—simple saint!
   Look! the Blood-Hounds are returning;
Lag's retreat was but a feint—
   On he comes for vengeance burning.
"Fly! all fly!" and how they fled—
   Is shown by hill and mountain passes—

---

[1] Grierson of Lag, whose relentless persecution of the Covenanters made his name infamous; and even to this day, it is abhorred by the peasantry of Dumfriesshire.

Hallowed cairns rise o'er the dead!
Where green for evermore the grass is!
For the FAITH they fought and fell—
Fell, but won immortal glory!
Seed then planted flourished well,
And deathless lives in Scottish story.

1877.

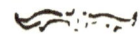

SANDY'S COMING.

SANDY'S coming—Sandy's coming:
Sandy soon will be at hame:
Bonnie birds the news are humming,
Echoes sound wi' Sandy's name!

Sandy's been where teeth are pearly,
Ebon black the polished skin,
Raven hair so crisp an' curly,
But their hearts are soft within.
Sandy's coming—Sandy's coming;
Sandy soon will be at hame:
Bonnie birds the news are humming,
Echoes sound wi' Sandy's name!

Sandy's hunted boundless prairies,
Countless miles ayont the sea;
He returns to sweet Glenairlies,
An' he comes to wed wi' me.
Sandy's coming—Sandy's coming;
Sandy soon will be at hame:
Bonnie birds the news are humming,
Echoes sound wi' Sandy's name!

Deck the porch wi' broon an' heather,
  On the lintels wreathe his name!
Berries red an' leaves thegether,
  Let him see he's welcome hame!
    Sandy's coming—Sandy's coming;
      Sandy soon will be at hame:
    Bonnie birds the news are humming,
      Echoes sound wi' Sandy's name!

Ilka thing wi' love is blending,
  On the hearth the cricket springs!
Cakes afore the fire are bending,
  On the hob the kettle sings!
    Sandy's coming—Sandy's coming;
      Sandy soon will be at hame:
    Bonnie birds the news are humming,
      Echoes sound wi' Sandy's name.

Hark! the merry bells are telling
  Sandy's noo upon the green;
Oh my heart, restrain your swelling,
  Half your joy maun no be seen!
    Sandy's coming—Sandy's coming;
      Sandy soon will be at hame:
    Bonnie birds the news are humming,
      Echoes sound wi' Sandy's name!

Sandy's come! Oh, joyous meeting,
  Sandy's foot is on the stair—
Steek the door on lovers' greeting—
  Sandy's hame for evermair.
    Sandy is nae mair a coming,
      Sandy's noo content at hame!
    Earth an' air his praises summing!
      Swell the chorus, Sandy's hame!

THE HIZZIES.

A SONG.

HEY for the hizzies sae bonny,
    I'll lo'e them as lang as I can:
O hey for the hizzies sae bonny,
    The pride and the comfort o' man.

Having wandered this warl'; the feck o't,
    This truth I am bound to declare,
Where womankind maist is respecket,
    That nation is freest frae care;
They are wilfu' and vain and hae failings,
    As a' things created maun hae:
But whaur wud be man and his ailings,
    Were womankind banished away.
        O hey for the hizzies sae bonny,
            I'll lo'e them as lang as I can:
        O hey for the hizzies sae bonny,
            The pride an' the comfort o' man.

There are linty, an' raven, an' red,
    Wi' sunny glint auburn an' broun,
Sleek braided or frizzed on the head,
    Or pinnacled high on the croun:

But whether brunetty or fair,
  Wi' figures, plump, rounded, or slim,
Had ADAM lived now I could swear
  Eve wand hae been jealous o' him.
    O hey for the hizzies sae bonny,
      I'll lo'e them as lang as I can;
    O hey for the hizzies sae bonny,
      The pride an' the comfort o' man.

Yestreen as I gaed to Drumslacket,
  I thought for my cousin I'd speer—
"Gin a kiss ye maun hae come an' tak' it,
  But no by that winnock so clear:
Hae dune wi' your daffin, Frank cousin—
  I offered ye ane, but instead
I am sure ye hae taken a dozen—
  A tee totum spins in my head."
    O hey for the hizzies sae bonny,
      I'll lo'e them as lang as I can;
    O hey for the hizzies sae bonny,
      The pride an' the comfort o' man.

O little thocht I that her mither,
  Was keeking ahint the ha' door,
Her voice put us baith in a swither,
  I felt as I'd sink through the floor:
"It's only our cousin frae Seaham,"
  The quick witted hizzie replied;
"Your answer, dear mither, come gie him,
  He's wanting to mak me his bride."
    O hey for the hizzies sae bonny,
      I'll lo'e them as lang as I can;
    O hey for the hizzies sae bonny,
      The pride an' the comfort o' man.

Gude lord, what a lie she was telling,
  But how could I say it was wrang,
I kenned she'd a bonny wee dwelling,
  An' maybe she'd lo'e me ere lang:
An' sae wi' a kiss I was hooket—
  Wha kens but my pleasures will double—
An' if as grey mare she is booket
  'Twill save me a hantle o' trouble!
    O hey for my hizzie sae bonny,
      I'll lo'e her as weel as I can;
    O hey for the hizzies are bonny,
      The pride an' subduer o' man.

1868.

MY AIN WIFE.

KEN ye no' my ain wife,
    Sae cheery, young, an' free;
O saw ye ne'er my ain wife,
    She's mair than gowd to me:
    Sae bonny, thrifty, neat, an' kind,
Sae fu' o' sense an' glee;
O wha kens no' my ain wife,
    Kens no' what wives should be!
    Sae patient, loving, blythe an' true,
    At least she's sae to me!
    O, I wadna gie my ain wife
    For ony wife I see!

Our hame, it is a cosey hame,
    Our garden is na sma';
My wife amang her blossoms, blooms
    The sweetest o' them a'.
The rose an' lily on her cheeks
    Are mingled baith sae fair,
I aften think the blushing things
    Hae found their beauty there:
    But she's mair sweet than sweetest flower,
    At least she's sae to me—
    O, I wadna gie my ain wife
    For ony wife I see!

The mavis on the sycamore,
  The lintie on the spray,
The laverock quivering up the sky,
  Sings sweet at break o' day.
O' ilka bird that ever sang
  On tree or joyous wing,
Wad cease its sweetest happy strain
  To hear my wifie sing;
    Sae fu' o' feeling is her voice,
      At least its sae to me,
    O, I wadna gie my ain wife
      For ony wife I see!

1870.

COMMEMORATIVE SONG.

COME, my wifie, come awa',
  And leave the Babel toun:
We'll gather flowers by Craigieha',
  Where Almond tummels doun—
Where Almond tummels doun, my love,
  And birdies frae the tree
Awake the echoes o' the grove,
  That tell o' love an' thee!

O listen! now the water sings
  A sang o' peace an' war,
As gliding where the ivy clings,
  Or dashing owre a scaur!
It tells how Scotia's poet king
  Defended was frae harm,
As now your heart, my bonnie thing,
  Is sheltered by my arm!

O days, an' weeks, an' years may glide
  Adoun life's troubled stream,
Some glints o' joy will still abide,
  Like mem'ries of a dream—

A dream foretelling happy days,
    O love! wi' fancy free:
I'll think of Almond's woody ways,
    O' Cramond glen, and thee.

1871.

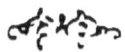

WHAT'S HER NAME?

IS it Aggy, or Agnes, or Nancy, or Nan?
    I heed not the name though I own that a spell
Is found in her presence—and envy the man
    Whose fortunate fate is beside her to dwell.

'Tis long, long ago since I watched her one morn,
    As she sat by her window o'ershadowed with care;
She thought of the absent, so lonely and lorn,
    And played with the braid of her glossy brown hair.

A single hair chosen, with twisting and twirl
    Around her fair finger a ring with it made,
Repeating the action, we envied the curl,
    But pitied the speck on her beautiful head!

Though years have flown o'er her, and changes have come,
 Her smiles and her dimples and roses remain;
'Tis sweet to behold her so joyous at home,
 Beloved by her friends, and so loving again!

1873.

WAE'S MY LIFE.

Il! wae's my life and sad my heart,
 The salt tears fill my eyes, Willie;
No hope can bloom this side the tomb,
 My songs are changed to sighs, Willie.
Of world's wealth I could not boast,
 But now I'm poor indeed, Willie;
The last fond hope I leant upon
 Has failed me in my need, Willie.

For wealth or fame thou'st left thy Jane,
 Forgot thy plighted vow, Willie;
Can honours proud dispel the cloud
 That darkens on thy brow, Willie?
Oh, was I then a thing so mean,
 For nought but beauty prized, Willie!
Caressed one day, then cast away,
 A faded flower despised, Willie.

Since love has fled, now hope is dead,
    Soon this poor heart will break, Willie;
As dear as life, oh, guard thy wife!
    I'll love her for thy sake, Willie.
Through my despair, a fervent prayer
    Will rise for her and thee, Willie;
That thou may'st prove to her in love
    More faithful than to me, Willie!

1852.

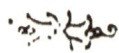

NANNIE BELL.

A SONG.

ILL luck to the time I hae tarried,
    Ill luck to the days that are gane;
The lasses are a' getting married,
    An' I am left cheerless alane.

O' bonnie anes mony I've seen,
    Wi' tresses as black as the craw;
Bewitching the glint o' their een,
    An' lips red an' ripe as a haw.
Bewildered my days hae been spent,
    I couldna wale ane frae the ither;
Alane I could say what I meant,
    But was dazed when I met them thegither.
    Ill luck on the time I hae tarried,
        Ill luck on the days that are gane;
    The lasses are a' getting married,
        An' I maun sit waesome alane.

There was hinny-mou'd Kate o' the hill,
    Wi' a neck like the eider-down saft,
I counted her mine,—but a chill
    Cam owre me ae nicht when she laughed,
An' ca'd me the ancient o' days;
    She thought me as auld as her mither!
Confessed she was proud o' my praise,
    But pointed to Matty M'Swither.
        Ill luck on the days I hae tarried,
            Ill luck on the days that are gane;
        The lasses are a' getting married,
            An' I maun sit cringing alane!

There's Aggy, the lass without taint,
    Nae'snaw on the riggin was clearer;
She looket sae muckle the saint
    That the evil one daur'd na come near her.
As modest, meek, shy as a dove,
    Sae jimpy, sae neat, an' sae snoddy!
Yet spurned she my heart for the sake
    O' a' short-necket minister body.
        Ill luck on the time I hae tarried,
            Ill luck on the days that are gane;
        The lassies are a' getting married,
            An' I maun sit sighing alane.

But whist! an' a secret I'll tell!
    When musing ae nicht in my chamour,
That hazel e'ed widow, NAN BELL,
    Cast owre me—O siccan a glamour.
She looket—I looket! She smiled—
    I smiled! But I'll no be confessing.

She clung to my breast like a child!
An' the minister gied us his blessing.
Oh, gude luck on the time I hae tarried,
Gude luck on the days that are gane,
Sin sweet NANNIE BELL I hae married,—
Oh sweet NANNIE BELL is my ain!

1868.

SONG.

STEEK the door, my bonnie lass,
And sit ye doun beside me;
I feel when near my bonnie lass
Nae evil can betide me.

Some happy years hae come and gaen
Sin' ye were bound to me, lass;
O wedded life is liberty,
'Twere bondage to be free, lass.
O, steek the door, my bonnie lass,
And sit ye doun beside me;
I feel when near my bonnie lass
Nae evil can betide me.

Nae sordid passion hoarding gear
Nae mean or miser part, lass,
Nae sterilizing atmosphere,
To shrivel up the heart, lass.
O, steek the door, my bonnie lass,
And sit ye doun beside me;
I feel when near my bonnie lass
Nae evil can betide me.

SONG.

Yestreen the storm blew fierce and loud,
    We trembled for our home, lass,
But morning broke without a cloud,
    Fortelling joys to come, lass.
        O, steek the door, my bonnie lass,
            And sit ye down beside me;
        I feel when near my bonnie lass
            Nae evil can betide me.

Should troubles come, or man oppress,
    To fret the heart wi' care, lass,
To feel your hand my hand caress
    Will drive away despair, lass.
        Sae steek the door, my bonny lass,
            And sit ye down to cheer me,
        I feel when near my bonnie lass
            Nae trouble can come near me.

1866.

SONG.

DINNA HINNER ME.

JOHN, but ye're an unco plague,
   An' winna bide awa':
At milkins, baith at nicht an' morn,
   I get nae peace ava.
Hae dune wi ye're daflin, John,
   Though unco nice it be:
Hae dune wi' ye're daflin, John,
   Ye sairlie hinner me.

The kail is boilin' owre the pat—
   There's tirlin' at the yett!
The milk it cruddles, when ye're near
   The butter winna set:
      O tak awa' your han', John,
         An' lettin' mine be free!
      O, tak' awa' your han, John,
         An' dinna hinner me!

Gae hund your collie at the stirks,
   They're doun amang the corn;

An' gin my minnie catches me,
  I'll hear o' it the morn !
      Sae tak awa your lips, John,
        An' patient bide awee ;
      O, tak awa your lips, John,
        An' let a lassie be !

In winter, when the sheep are fauled,
  The kye within the byre,
And when the minister has been,
  Ye'se hae your heart's desire :
      Ye'll hae your heart's desire, John,
        An' sae will I in thee ;
      When ance the twain are ane, John,
        We need na hinnert be !

1875.

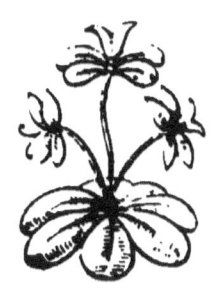

I WILL LIPPEN THEE, LASSIE.

SONG.

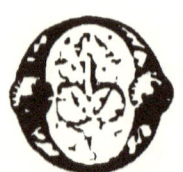
I will lippen thee, lassie,
   I will lippen thee!
O, I will lippen thee, lassie,
   For ye lippen me!

What matters gin your father's dour,
   When, Jessie, thou art fain!
What matters gin your minnie's sour,
   Sin', lassie, thou'rt my ain!
      O, I will lippen thee, lassie,
         I will lippen thee!
      O, I will lippen thee, lassie,
         For ye lippen me!

O did the auld anes ever love,
   An' do as lovers do?
I trow me no, for gin they had
   Mair feeling they wad shew.
      O, I will lippen thee, lassie,
         I will lippen thee!
      O, I will lippen thee, lassie,
         For ye lippen me!

To think true love should only prove
    A feather in the air,
An' rowth o' land assent command,
    Mak's worthy men despair!
        But I will lippen thee, lassie,
            I will lippen thee!
        But I will lippen thee, lassie,
            For ye lippen me!

In Edintown some pawky loon
    Entangled in your smile,
May, like a man, do all he can
    Your heart frae me to wile.
        But I will lippen thee, lassie,
            I will lippen thee!
        But I will lippen thee, lassie,
            For ye lippen me!

Fareweel a while—we'll meet in Kyle,
    Whatever some may say;
Our love sincere will keep us near,
    Though thou art far away.
        Sae I will lippen thee, lassie,
            I will lippen thee!
        Sae I will lippen thee, lassie,
            For ye lippen me!

Thy countless charms within my arms
    I fauld wi' kisses sweet;
Twa waiting years o' hopes an' fears
    Our triumph makes complete.
        'Twas weel I lippened thee, lassie.
            Jessie bricht an' free;
        I ever lippened thee, lassie,
            For ye lippened me.

1875.

ISA.

OH! it's bonnie, bonnie Isa,
    Whose hair is like the craw,
Her e'e the dusky violet,
    Her neck the drifted snaw:
By hills an' howes where Annan rowes
    Are lasses bricht an' braw,
But my bonnie, bonnie Isa
    Is the flower amang them a'.

I lo'ed her in the summer time,
    When sweet the laverock sang;
And mair an' mair in winter prime,
    When nichts were dark and lang:
But oh, I lo'ed her maist o' a'
    When, nestlin' near tae me,
She pined awa—owre plain I saw
    My bonnie bairn wad dee.

She took my hans atween her ain,
    An' held them tae her breast,
An' wi' her slender fingers, mine
    Sae tenderly caressed;

Then lookin' up sae lovingly,
  While tears cam' rinnin' doon,
Said, " Willie!—Willie, think o' me!
  I'll be in heaven soon."

But while she spak' a stranger cam'—
  (Then melted was the snaw)—
Said, " Isa will arise again,
  An' be a joy tae a'."
An' in the spring our Isa rose,
  Slipped aff her weary pain;
An' smilin' bricht as simmer light,
  She's brocht us joy again!

1870.

ON RECEIVING A BUNCH OF VIOLETS, CHRISTMAS, 1869.

HE frost had fettered stream and lake,
The silent snow fell flake on flake,
Though wold and field were all unseen,
We knew the grass was growing green.

Low fell the drooping curtain cloud,
And veiled the sky as with a shroud;
Yet far beyond—we knew the light
Of Glory shone, with radiance bright!

When, chilled with cold, and fingers numb,
I saw the welcome missive come;
The hidden flowers sweet odours bring,
To tell me somewhere breathes the spring.

In every trusting heart is found
Some little patch of sacred ground,
Where flowers of Faith and Hope have room
To spread and shed a sweet perfume.

GLEN VALENTINE.[1]

COME, bonnie lassie—come away!
In shady woods we'll spend the day,
And in the evening slowly stray
　　To beautiful Glen Valentine.
When lambkins bleat along the hill,
And evening dews their sweets distil,
We'll every sense with rapture fill
　　In beautiful Glen Valentine.

---

[1] This secluded and beautiful glen may be found among the grassy hills of Upper Nithsdale. The pedestrian from Thornhill to Leadhills, passing up Carron Water, will arrive at Dalveen House, and cross the ridge of hill immediately behind that pleasant residence. Having descended into the bottom of the glen, and beginning to ascend towards Leadhills, he will come, on the right hand, to a glen which meets Glen Enterkin at nearly right angles. This is Glen Valentine, which winds round the base of the beautiful hills. So silent is it, that beyond it one might fancy he could find the Fountain of Eternal Silence. Near the foot of the glen is a scaur, most picturesque and wonderfully tinted: all shades of yellow and violet, up to the deepest red, may be seen there; and there stand sundry rocks, like monuments of the past, protesting against the bloody wars, to which tradition ascribes the glowing colours referred to.

GLEN VALENTINE.

Whoe'er goes there, by day or night,
By sunshine or by starry light,
There ever beams a radiance bright
    In beautiful Glen Valentine.
There rises high the tinted scaur,
Bloodstained in time of Clavers' war;
Its hues remain, though strife afar
    Is banished from Glen Valentine.

The Clyde may boast its Cora Linn;
The Nith its tawny foam and din;
The neighbouring glen its Enterkin;
    Give me serene Glen Valentine.
High o'er my head the curlew calls,
Where mountains rise like grassy walls;
Beside me sing the waterfalls
    Of beautiful Glen Valentine.

And here, to cheer me, dawns a smile,
And swells a bosom free from guile—
A hand within my hand the while
    Makes beautiful Glen Valentine.
Whilst Lowthers lifts its lofty brow,
Dalveen spreads green its bonny knowe,
I'll sacred keep the solemn vow
    First breathed in sweet Glen Valentine.

1869.

TO MY MOTHER,

ON ATTAINING HER EIGHTY-THIRD YEAR OF AGE.

HAPPY new year! my Mother;
 A happy and healthy new year!
Many years have flown over us, Mother,
 Since New Year's day found me here.

Though many a change has come, Mother;
 For thankfulness—how much room!
Though half of the joy of your life, Mother,
 Lies low in the silent tomb.

It is thirty years and more, Mother,—
 The time I remember well:
The frost was hard in the vale, Mother,
 The snow lay deep on the fell:

The drift drove high o'er the hill, Mother,
 And ships were wrecked in the bay:
And cattle, and sheep, and men, Mother,—
 Were lost on that sorrowful day.

TO MY MOTHER.

When the wild winds ceased to wail, Mother,
    And neighbours in sympathy met,
To speak of the touching tale, Mother,—
    A tale I can never forget:

The Minister in the Kirk, Mother,
    Wept sore when he tried to bless;
But, oh, how he fervently prayed, Mother,
    For widowed and fatherless!

The time has long passed and gone, Mother,
    Like a stone dropped into the sea,
But low in the core of my heart, Mother,
    'Tis written, and present with me!

Then—then, like the raven's wing, Mother,
    My hair was black;—but now,
Time's wintry frost and rime, Mother,
    Lie white upon cheek and brow.

'Tis a wearisome life at best, Mother,
    But lessons of love and truth
Are seldom forgotten in age, Mother,
    When properly taught in youth.

So tutored we welcome death, Mother,
    And lovingly go to rest
On the balmy bosom of earth, Mother,
    As a bird returns to its nest.

And now I must off and away, Mother:
    In going I can but pray
God's blessing may rest on your head, Mother,
    This beautiful New Year's day.

IN MEMORIAM.

TEN years ago, in summer time,
  In peace we gently laid him,
Where chestnut, oak, and beech combine
  Their woven boughs to shade him.

To shade, not him, but what remained:
  The soul, the body spurning,
Had flown away to realms of day,
  Dust waiting its returning.

And now the sere leaves, fading, fall.
  In every tread we feel them
To crunching break, as if they'd speak,
  Where eddying breezes wheel them.

The sun showers heat from azure skies,
  No cloud flings darkness o'er us.
The only shadow darkling near
  Comes from the bier before us.

Deep, deep in earth a father lies!—
  Two sisters and a brother
Repose on either side,—and now
  We gently lay a mother!

'Tis well; for fifty years or more
  They fought life's fight together,
And shared its perils, griefs, and joys,
  Its rough, its peaceful weather.

One aim in life, one hope in death,
  Was year by year unfolding—
Then came decay, they pass away,
  One grave their dust is holding!

No higher aim than honest fame—
  Their trust, the Gospel story;
They gently fell asleep in faith,
  To wake again in glory!

1870.

THE BRUISED FLOWER.

 HE stripping wind blew howling past,
    And quivering, from the poplars tall
The whirling leaves fell thick and fast,
    And eddying flew to hedge and wall
    For refuge ere the rain should fall.

The drenching rain came down apace,
    Down came the stinging arrowy sleet;
When Susan, with a streaming face,
    With tattered gown, and naked feet,
    Came shivering slowly up the street;

Came battling with the driving rain,
    With burning brow and bosom bare—
Shelter was proffered—pressed—'twas vain—
    While spurning back her matted hair
    She cried, " What shelters from despair?"

She heedless passed her birthplace by,
    And staggering, crept the old church round:
Then lingering, fixed her wandering eye
    A moment on a little mound—
    A baby's grave—sad verdict—"drowned!"

A traitorous tongue with flattery wooed
    And won her heart—then stole her dower,
Her honey-dew of maidenhood:
    In pain—in her extremest hour—
    He flung away the bruised flower!

The tempest ceased, the morn arose—
    Men rose to glean late autumn sheaves;
And where the whispering poplar grows,
    And plaintive wind perpetual grieves,
    Half-buried by the withering leaves,

Lay one released from scorn—from strife;
    Her cold hand clenched this scroll, which saith,—
"O God! forgive him in his life
    As I forgive him in my death;
    And, oh! forgive my sinning faith."

RETRIBUTIVE.

On last year's graves the grass is green,
    And marriage-bells are gaily ringing—
A courtly knight has bridegroom been,
    And all the world his praise is singing,—
    But close—how close the bride is clinging!

White as the snowy wreath she wears—
    Her breathing quick, her step unsteady:
Haste, haste—she faints! what anguish tears
    His soul? Too late—too late! already
    On Susan's grave lies dead his lady!

OVER THE HILLS.

OVER the hills the wintry wind
    Blew wildly, fiercely screaming;
Adown the glen rushed tawny floods,
The tempest rocked the Closeburn
      woods,
    Where lay the cushats dreaming:
And dreaming, too, a maiden lay,
A maiden lovely as the day,
'And sweet as is the scented May,
    Lay Hebe fondly dreaming.

Over the hills the spring winds came,
    Softly, gently blowing:
Adown the glen the glancing rills
Came dancing from the Closeburn hills,
    In sweetest cadence flowing:
And down the glen a gallant came,
Who woke to life love's latent flame,
New life awakened by a name
    That came like music flowing.

Over the hills the summer breeze
    Came with odours laden;
Odours wafted from the trees,
Where sing the happy summer bees,
    And happy made the maiden:
For with it came sweet orange flowers,
So wisely prized in lady bowers;
Oh, Hebe is no longer ours,
    For married is the maiden!
  1862.

THE MAID OF ALTON VALE.

AMID the rocky sylvan scene
    Where murmuring Churnet flows,
With many a curve through meadows green,
    'Neath cliffs with beetling brows,
Young Bertha, like a flower of spring
    Unfolding, pleased the eye;
Her voice could cheer like sweetest song,
    Or melt like summer's sigh.

As seasons flew, the maiden grew
    So wonderfully fair,
That many a loving youth was drawn
    To watch and wander there.
But there was one of lordly state,
    Who prayed he might prevail,
And win to grace his sisterhood
    The maid of Alton Vale.

With wily speech and holy zeal,
    And dazzling promise blent,
Bewildered Bertha trembling gave
    A whispering, slow consent.
Soon, soon the roses on her cheeks
    Were changed for lilies pale,
And many a pitying heart bemoaned
    The maid of Alton Vale.

For saintly vows the Abbess thought
    The novice inly pined,
Nor dreamt that Bertha's beating heart
    To other vows inclined.—
The rock was steep, the turret high,
    Yet love found means to scale :
By Harry's side she blooms a bride.
    And still in Alton Vale.

1856.

MARY.

THE vernal blossoms, budding fair,
    Were not so fair as Mary;
The sweetest sounds that charm the air
    Were far excelled by Mary.
Her looks awoke the poet's strain;
He looked, admired, and looked again:
The wisdom beaming from her brain
    Made sages yield to Mary!

The summer breathing odours sweet
    Were ever sweet to Mary,
And Autumn made her joy complete;
    So happy then was Mary!
Young Love was cherished in her breast:
Her lover's wishes all confessed,
Within his arms supremely blessed,
    Most blessed of maids was Mary!

But winter's chilling blasts have come,
    And winter's come to Mary;
Black desolation marks the home
    Of once the blithesome Mary!

All weary now she sits alone;
Friends dearest—kindred—all are gone;
The sleepless night-wind's plaintive moan
   Companion is of Mary!

THE PIPING SHEPHERD BOY.

INSCRIBED TO JENNY L——.

WE musing wandered by the streams
   That glide through grassy vales,
Between the mountains high and green
   Of ever-pleasant Wales;
And, listening, heard such music flow
   As filled the ear with joy!
Instinctively we praised the cause—
   A piping shepherd boy!

The strain in softest cadence told
   A tender tale of love,
More sweet than song of nightingale,
   Or linnet in the grove;
Rock, stream, and lake their echoes wake
   And waver o'er the plain—
Its trem'lous movements swell the heart,
   And linger in the brain.

It changed! and then its thrilling tones
   Made vibrate chords of fire,
To rouse the patriotic soul,
   And daring deeds inspire!
We seemed to hear the measured tread
   Of troops of marching men;
With fife and drum, they bannered come
   In triumph through the glen!

Another change! How sweet and strange!
   We feel our cheeks grow pale;
Great tears arise and dim our eyes,
   The march becomes a wail
Of deepest grief for maid or chief,
   Then, fading with the day,
Far up the hill, where mists are chill,
   The music dies away.

1875.

A POET'S WIFE.

HE slept when fever had racked his brain,
  And wildering visions alarmed his soul;
While sleeping, he felt that the holiest strain
  Of melody over his senses stole:
    It calmed his breast, it soothed his brow,
    Its memory haunts him even now.

He dreamt, and a spirit that cheered like wine
  Appeared in the shape of a witching flower:
And from its chalice a hand divine
  Poured odorous dew in a ceaseless shower:
    It cooled his cheek, made glad his heart,
    And he felt new life in his pulses start.

Oh, still he dreamt, and the magical thing
  Assumed the form of a meek-eyed dove;
And the breeze it flung from its fluttering wing
  Was the heavenly breath of sustaining love:
    Through every nerve it quickening ran,
    From a trance like death he awoke a man.

He awoke, and beside his weary bed,
  To smooth his pillow and fan his cheek,
Watched one whose beauty his dreams had fed—
  Whose presence gave strength to his frame so weak:
    Unwearying love had saved his life,—
    'Twas Rosa, his beautiful, patient wife.
1854.

A POET'S DAUGHTER.

YOUNG Rosa is bonny, and blithe, and gay,
As a sunny gleam on a showery day,
Or the firstling flower of the sweet, sweet May.

Like music, when wedded to words of sense;
Like truth, unsullied by vain pretence;
She is melody, mirth, and innocence.

As the pool leaps up when the rain-drops fall,
Her spirit leaps up when the sorrowing call:
Where pain is felt, she would soothe it all.

To merit all eyes, and to rudeness blind,
Rejoicing in all that she good can find;
"For the darkest cloud is with silver lined."

Her laugh is merry, and clear, and shrill
As the hunter's horn when the air is still,
Or the lark when it carols o'er cloud and hill.

Oh, she is not fair; for her dark hair shines
In twisted masses—her cheek inclines
To the brown warm hue of the land of vines.

Her mother looks out from her coal-black eyes,
And her father's spirit is seen to rise
When they kindle and flash with a quick surprise.

Not alone for her beauty and gentle mood
Is Rosa beloved as one's daily food;
We love her—all love her—because she's good.

NEVER DESPAIR.

AGAIN I behold thee, green gem of the ocean,
   Revisit the home where I wandered a child,
   But what makes my heart feel this tremulous motion?
My house is deserted, my garden a wild!
Yet I will not despair. Sure the fond love I cherish
   Shall urge me to action, my house to repair;
No more I'll forsake thee—no! sooner I'll perish
   Than fail in my duty, and faint in despair!

Where are the ties of affection that bound me,
   Where is Aileen, I have come back to wed?
Like the leaves of the autumn they're scattered around me,
   My friends they have vanished—poor Aileen is dead!

Yet I grieve not, believe not but pleasure seeds
    flying
  May lodge in my heart and grow blossoming
    there!—
Sure love like a branch duly grafted in season,
  Will yield me its fruit—so I will not despair.

Oh, love, darling love, in its truth never changes,
  Its object may fade and its subject may die,
'Tis the spirit of life, through creation it ranges,
  The pulse of the earth and the light of the sky.
Oh, I will not repine; far beyond the storms drearest
  In beauty serene, smiles a sky ever fair!
So behind the heart's grief lies the love that is
    dearest,
  Who woos it shall win it. Oh, never despair.

    1852.

TO NATHANIEL HAWTHORNE.

ON THE ANNIVERSARY OF HIS DAUGHTER UNA'S BIRTHDAY.

VERSE!—My friend, 'tis hard to rhyme
   When cares the heart enfold,
And Fancy feels the freezing time,
   And shrivels with the cold.
' And yet, however hard it seems
   To generously comply,
The heart, fraternal, throbbing, deems
   It harder to deny.

Few love the weary Winter time,
   When trees are gaunt and bare,
And fields are grey with silver rime,
   And biting keen the air.
Though all without is weird and waste,
   And shrill the tempest's din,
With those well suited to our taste
   How bright is all within!

But oh! the Spring, the early Spring,
   Is brimming full of mirth,
When mating birds, on happy wing,
   Rain music on the earth;
And Earth, responsive, spreadeth wide
   Her leafy robe of green,
Till March is wreathed in flowery pride—
   A smiling virgin queen.

Oh! that dear time is dearer made
   By Love's mysterious will,
Which in the sun and in the shade
   Its impulse must fulfil;
In wood, or wild, or rosy face,
   The law is broad and clear;
Love lends its all-entrancing grace
   To spring-time of the year.

Spring-time, my friend, with mystic words,
   Has filled thy life with joy,
Bound close thy heart with triple cords
   That age can ne'er destroy.
For her, thy first—so fair, so good,
   So innocent and sweet—
An angel pure as model stood!
   The copy, how complete!

Oh! sacred season, ever blest,
   When saints their offerings bring,
Thou to thy heart an offering prest
   More fair than flowers of Spring.

A miracle!—long ere the yoke
  Of winter passed away,
Thy Hawthorne into blossom broke,
  Anticipating May! [1]

---

[1] The foregoing verses were composed at the urgent request of the late Nathaniel Hawthorne, my intimate and very dear friend, on the anniversary of the birthday of his daughter Una. Hence the allusion in the last verse, which, without this explanation, would not be understood. The verses were written several years ago. Mr. Hawthorne was then staying at Leamington, in Warwickshire, busy with the last sheets of his Italian romance "Transformation." In the words of a relative, "The verses bring up many pleasant recollections, dimmed by the remembrance that he, who could rouse with a skill unequalled the tenderest emotions, and depict with infinite power the deepest passions of the human heart, is mouldering in the tomb. Those who knew Mr. Hawthorne best loved him most: and all who were acquainted with the plans he had hoped to carry out, regret that death should have stilled the heart and stayed the hand before his greatest work was accomplished."

A SKETCH FROM MEMORY.

FORGET her! ah, no, I shall never
    forget her;
  How silently, fondly enraptured
    I clung
    To the soul-soothing cadence first
      heard when I met her,
The syllabled sweetness that flowed from her
    tongue!

Her brow so illumined by goodness and wit is,
  Her cheeks blushing beauty unfurrowed by
    care;
Her eye beaming love with all tenderness lit is;
  And lips made for kissing;—I wonder who'd
    dare!

So lithesome and graceful, reclining or moving,
  So light is her footfall, we hear not a sound;
A womanly woman, with spirit all loving,
  We feel as she walks we should envy the
    ground;

In toil or in leisure, her love without measure
  Would comfort and gladden the heart of a
      man;
A fathomless pleasure—an evermore treasure—
  Is found in our peerless—our sweet *Marianne*.

1867.

WHAT LOVE IS LIKE.

LOVE is like the forest glade,
At once a shelter and a shade,
From autumn wind and winter snow,
And hectic summer's passion glow:
    O! my love is like the forest
      glade,
    At once a shelter and a shade.

O! Love is like the orange tree,
On which both flower and fruit we see;
Buddings sweet, and fruitage green,
Mingling with the ripe are seen.
    O! my love is like the orange tree,
    Bringing flowers and fruit to me.

O! Love is like the monthly rose,
That neither spring nor winter knows;
Month by month it blossom strews,
Month by month its bud renews.
    O! my love is like the blushing rose,
    That neither spring nor winter knows.

WHAT LOVE IS LIKE.

O! Love is like the eager bee,
And gathers sweets from wood and lea,
From purple heath—acacia bloom,
And clover shedding sweet perfume;
    O! my love is like the restless bee,
    And sweetest honey brings to me.

O! Love is like a streamlet bright
That laughs beneath the starry light,
And, dancing gaily, singing goes
To clasp the ocean whence it rose!
    O! were my love as streamlets are,
    I'd be—but not a distant—star!

O! Love is like the eddying breeze,
That bears the odour from the trees,
Or, lingering, toys with every grace,
And clasps the world in soft embrace.
    O! my love is like the winds that play,
    And clasps me closer day by day.

O! Love is like the bird that flies
Evermore to sunny skies,
Shuns the storm, and seeks the charm
Of shady groves, in regions warm;
    O, my love is like a bird, and flies
    To bask beneath his lady's eyes.

1867.

FAIR AND BRIEF.

AIR and brief—fair and brief,
Opening flower and swelling leaf,
Beautiful beyond belief
Are the summer's flower and leaf.

Loving eyes—loving eyes,
Glancing with a new surprise;
On her knee the baby lies,
Ah! how soon the spirit flies!

Joy and grief—joy and grief,
Mingling, make this mortal sheaf!
Comes the worm, and, like a thief,
Steals the beauty from the leaf!

Paling cheek—paling cheek,
Parching lip and hectic streak,
Sleepless eyes and pulsings weak,
Sapping sickness plainly speak!

Ah! how brief—ah, how brief!
Time and change brought no relief
From the sentence! Woe and grief!—
She died, as died the autumn leaf.

AN APPEAL FOR PEACE.[1]

DURING THE FRANCO-GERMAN WAR.

O LUST of Conquest, Power, and Fame,
    Ambition, Wealth, and Pride!
What evils follow in your train;
    For you have millions died!
Alas! alas! for bonny France!
    Her rivers Loire and Seine
Run red with blood; their sunny banks
    Are reeking with the slain.

O Europe, lift your mighty voice,
    And bid the carnage cease!
From out thy sea-walled citadel,
    O England, plead for peace!
Plead for the helpless, homeless ones,
    Childhood and hoary years;
Plead for the orphan's piteous cry,
    The wailing widow's tears!

---

[1] Set to music and sold for the benefit of the Refugees' Benevolent Fund.

Republic, Council, Kaiser-King,
    Forget not this DECREE!
Each loving life your lust destroys,
    Heaven will demand of thee!
Command, O GOD, Thou King of kings,
    Break angry passions down:
That PEACE, and LOVE, and BROTHERHOOD
    May all the nations crown!

1870.

LINES WRITTEN DURING ILLNESS.

ROUND our home the winter's storm
    Its fearful conflict wages,
While in my poor devoted frame
    Intensest fever rages:
But storm without, nor fire within,
    Can sink the heart in sadness,
Or change the sunshine of my life
    To melancholy madness!

Untiring love upon me waits,
    A wife's devout attention,
And every want anticipates
    Ere lips their wish can mention:
While love remains, the bed of pain
    Is changed to one of pleasure,
It tries the truth of early vows,
    And proves the heart a treasure.

When Nature gave my love her life,
   She then brought forth her fairest;
When Fortune gave her as a wife,
   She gave me then her rarest;
And to protect her while I may
   Shall be my chief endeavour,
With love that strengthens day by day,
   And only Death can sever!

LOVE'S POTENCY.

Oh, heavy pain!—Oh, weary brain!
   Oh, heart that wildly beateth!
Great ocean's surge, love's moaning dirge
   For evermore repeateth
The dismal cry—from earth to sky—
"Torn spirit, free thyself and fly!"

What, craven be! No, by the sea,
   And earth with all its treasures!
If she can scoff, then I can laugh,
   And seek some nobler pleasures.
Though she's divine, shall I repine?
No! Love and grief I'll drown in wine.

Oh, fool!—Oh, shame on manhood's name!
   Farewell to peace for ever;
I thought to drown Love's angry frown
   In wine as in a river.
I madly quaffed—at every draught
The fiends exultant mouthed and laughed.

The frenzy fled—around my head
 And in my heart sung angel voices,
"Be gentle, kind, and true, and find
 There's one in all thy joy rejoices."
Love's light did shine—I woke from wine,
And found my darling's hand in mine!

MY SPIRIT LOVE.

BY shady rocks, where trees grew tall,
 And near a sounding waterfall—
 When summer sweetest blossoms strewed,
 And birds melodious charmed the wood,
A maiden, meek as cooing dove,
I met, and told her all my love!

Adown her shoulders rippling rolled
Her wavy hair, like streams of gold!
From dewy eyes of azure hue,
A soul serene came beaming through.
My heart in cadence could but move
In unison with her I love!

The red rose and the lily strove
To win the cheek of my dear love;
The red rose did at first prevail,
But yielded to the lily pale!
And now? Ah me! in realms above
The lily crowns my Spirit Love!

1872.

EXILE'S SONG,

SUGGESTED BY A PICTURE PRESENTED TO THE AUTHOR BY THE COMMITTEE OF THE REFUGEES' BENEVOLENT FUND.

Sing, sing me the song of my Fatherland,
    That I left so long ago;
    And play me again that sweet old strain,
        With cadence soft and low!
Before my eyes dear mountains rise,
    And loom through the mist of years;
My grand old home, with turret and dome,
    Is glimmering through my tears.
        Sing, sing me the song of my Fatherland,
        That I left so long ago;
        And play me again that sweet old strain,
        With cadence soft and low!

List! list to the sound! for methinks I hear
    Far off the echoing horn!
And the hunter's call, that aroused us all
    For the chase on the breezy morn!

EXILE'S SONG.

Away, away fly the hunters gay,
   How gallantly on they ride !
But none of them all is so fair and tall,
   As Lillie, my own, my bride.
      Sing, sing me the song of my Fatherland,
        That I left so long ago :
      And play me again that sweet old strain,
        With cadence soft and low !

Hark ! hark, 'tis the beat of the rolling drum,
   And the hurrying rush of men !
O little cares Might for the cause of Right,
   Our freedom is stabbed again !
The vision has fled, and my weary head
   I lean on my feeble hand—
No more ! no more, O never more !
   Shall I gaze on my Fatherland.
      Yet sing me the song of my Fatherland.
        That I left so long ago ;
      O play me again the dear old strain,
        Though it maketh my tears to flow.

1872.

WELCOME IS NIGHT.

WELCOME is night, trebly welcome to him
Whose heart with love throbbing is full to the brim,
When the soul that's been fettered by care through the day,
On the pinions of pleasure soars sailing away;
When truth is most daring, most freely expressed,
O then let us drink to the friends we love best:
O now let us drink to the friends we love best!

Again fill a bumper—when woman's the theme!
Fill high! do not stint her, man's blessing supreme;
Whose voice in soft melody comes like a sigh
Of the balmy south wind, when the summer is nigh,
Which awakens the passion of love in his breast;
Now, now let us drink unto her we love best,
O now let us drink unto her we love best!

The earth has no beauty, nor fragrance, nor flowers,
If it drinks not—and deeply—of sunshine and showers:

So truth, love, and friendship, heart blossoms
    divine,
Grow fairest and dearest when nourished with
    wine,
Shall a man let them wither and die in his breast?
No! drink, brothers, drink, unto all we love best,
O drink, brothers, drink, unto all we love best!

THE TIDE WILL TURN.

THE tide rushed rapidly down to the
    sea,
  When the hurricane swept with
    wind and rain :
  Brave men on the shore waited pa-
tiently
  For a lull—when the tide would flow again ;
No wonder the mariner's heart should yearn
For the wind to cease and the tide to turn

The tide has turned, and across the bay
    The waves came rolling in crests of foam .
Out in the offing the great ship lay,
    Awaiting the breeze to waft her home ;
How pleasant to feel, though afar we roam,
Some loving one waits with a " Welcome home !"

THE TIDE WILL TURN.

The tide has turned—the merchant sighs
    When troublesome adverse winds had blown;
Messages sent, but no replies,
    How small a return for so much sown!
All imperilled that life has earned,
Thank Heaven, kind Heaven, the tide has turned.

The tide has turned, the lover may say,
    When wearily waiting the faintest sign
To give him some hope: O the darkest day
    Is illumined by rays that seem divine,
When the hand of love is no longer spurned:
He blesses his fate, for the tide has turned.

And so through every phase of life,
    Its chance, its change, its light and shade!
If true to ourselves, the battle and strife
    But strengthen the faith that hope has laid;
How sweet is the lesson of life thus learned,
When we see and feel that the tide has turned.

Though many are false, oh! more are true:
    Have faith in humanity, come what may;
There ever smiles over an arch of blue,
    Though clouds o'erspreading make dark our day:
Though sorrow may soften, or anger burn,
Have faith in the future—the tide will turn!

    1863.

THREE MEETINGS.

MET her first beside the stream,
    When music filled the evening breeze!
A fitting place to muse and dream
    Of life—beneath acacia trees;
And pacing fondly by her side,
Was one, her joy, her future guide.

To meet, salute—salute and part!—
    Was but an instant, scarce a word
Was spoken; yet within my heart
    Was touched a sympathetic chord
That time to friendship must mature—
A friendship mutual and secure.

When next we met, a mother's thought
    Through every movement clearly shone,
Expanding spheres of duty brought
    New powers to light, before unknown;
Her well-developed form and face
Embodied all of matron grace.

So calm, confiding, sweet her smile,
    We charmed beneath its influence lie:
No curl of scorn, no glance of guile,
    Affects the lip, or dims the eye.
Evolving from a soul sincere
A purifying atmosphere.

Again we met, and o'er her brow
    Was cast a shade of wifely care,
A moment dim—it passed—and now
    The cloud has melted into air;
Thus morning dews sun-kissed appear,
She looked the lovelier for the tear.

Our meetings, partings, joy and pain
    Make up this mingled woof of life:
We part, yet hope to meet again,
    And hope invigorates for strife:
The strife o'ercomes, and love's renewed
By deeds of kindly brotherhood.

1865.

WALLISSELLEN.

(NEAR ZURICH.)

UT! o'er the hills at break of day,
When merry maids were making hay,
And singing birds made glad the way,
    As I drove o'er to Wallissellen.
    I thought of friends, so true, so rare,
Of one as good as she is fair,
And wished that she were with me where
    The streamlet glides to Wallissellen.

'There countless fingers twist and twine
The filmy fibres that combine
To form a glistening silken line:—
    Of wedded life a happy token.
When hearts akin by nature led,
The path of life, as one, to tread:
Poor life! unlike a silken thread,
    Can ne'er be knit when once 'tis broken.

Humbly at first must all begin
Their aimless threads of life to spin,
Too often marred by gouts of sin!
    And all in dust appears as ended.

Ah, no! angelic fingers fine,
With wondrous skill, will find and twine
Each missing thread and all combine,
    Until in heaven again they're blended.

As every stream on earth with care
Must its own channel fret, and tear
Its way through hardest rocks, and bear
    Down to the sea its earthy leaven!
So man through life encounters still
Each form and shade of earthly ill,
And bears them in his soul until
    Pure life to him through death is given.

'Tis wise and good to musing sit
And note the varying thoughts that flit
Across the brain—such here are writ,—
    As homeward bound from Wallissellen.
All without order or design,
Like floating flakes in ambient wine,
I weave these random thoughts of mine
    Memorially of Wallissellen.

1865.

WRITTEN FOR THE PICTURE OF THE DUCHESS

OF ARGYLE AND HER SON THE

MARQUIS OF LORNE.

DAUGHTER of Sutherland, gentle and beautiful,
 Wife of the noble and gallant Argyle!
Mother of many hearts happy and dutiful,
'Blessed in thy presence and cheered with thy smile!
 England is proud of thee,
 Scotland speaks loud of thee,
Songs in thy praise on the breezes are borne,
 Sung by true-hearted men.
 Wafted o'er hill and glen,
"Health to Argyle and the Marquis of Lorne!"

The time has long passed since, with bonnet and feather,
Argyle with his clan like a tempest arose,

And swept from his mountains, like dew from the
    heather,
  The legions that ventured his power to oppose!
    The pibroch no more alarms;
    No longer calls to arms;
Nations that battled are blended as one;
    Peace and security,
    Love in its purity,
Flow from one Sceptre like light from the sun.

Yet, times may arise when the people will call on
  The boy that clings fondly and close to thy side
To guard them from peril—from evils that fall on
  A nation when gold is its idol of pride;
    Train him up kindly—
    Wisely, not blindly—
Teach him the duties to which he is born:
    The hope of the Highlands
    The pride of the Lowlands,
May centre on Thee and the Marquis of
    Lorne!

"*Keepsake,*" 1856.

NEIL GOW'S OAK.[1]

A VISION.

THE sun had set, the air was still,
    And slowly closed the day;
No breezy sound came from the hill,
    Nor murmur from the Tay:
I musing gazed upon the Oak,
    Beneath whose branches high,
Neil Gow from slumbering silence woke
    The soul of melody.

Deep darkness like a curtain came,
    I closed my weary eyes:

---

[1] The oak pointed out to tourists, as that under which Neil Gow was wont to sit and compose some of those wondrous melodies which have immortalized the songs of Scotland. Tradition states that Burns and Neil Gow met at Dunkeld. But be that as it may, it is indisputable that the spirits of the two men are for ever blended together by the words of the one and the music of the other.

On the Athole side of the river is a shaded seat where the Duke of Athole is said to have sat unseen, and listened to the music, without disturbing the popular performer on the violin.

Around the tree shone sparks of flame,
    Like stars in wintry skies.
Each acorn cup appeared a lamp,
    Each bough a harp was made
With gossamer strings; and over all
    Bent Neil's immortal shade.

A breeze crept up from Murthly woods,
    And swept the airy strings,
Till music swelled, like mountain floods,
    From all their secret springs;
And while the cadence ebbed and flowed,
    Clouds sympathizing wept,
The trees their topmost branches swayed,
    And faultless measure kept.

Soon through the hazy southern gloom,
    With halo round his head,
The shades of Burns approached—to whom
    The minstrel homage paid.
The poet, musing, caught the strains,
    And gave to sound sublime
The immortality of words,
    To charm through endless time.

I heard the stately solemn air
    That fires the patriot's soul,
And that which lifts from deep despair,
    And crowns the social bowl.
I saw the secret whisper breathed,
    I heard fond passion's vows,
And then a spray descending wreathed
    The bard and minstrel's brows.

I know not when the music ceased;
  I woke, but all was still,
The golden glory of the east
  Was gilding Birnam hill.
The Duke of Atholl I invoke,
  As he would honoured be,
To guard with care that sacred oak—
  Great Neil's immortal tree.

WATCHING AND WAITING.

FOR a weary year and a day, yestreen,
  Has Ronald, my Ronald, a rover been;
  And to-day—to-day he promised to come
  And visit my lovable mountain home;
  The day has faded—the stars appear,
Yet Ronald, my Ronald, is nowhere near!

The moonbeams whitened her brow so fair,
And rippled with light her nut-brown hair;
Twin stars looked down from azuline skies
And mirrored themselves in her hazel eyes;
As she strove with her palms on her heaving breast
To steady her heart in its great unrest!

She looked from her lattice, looked out on the night,
And looked on the silvery lake so bright,—

Then far away on its wavy tide,
As she eagerly peered was a sail descried,
Which nearer and clearer approached the strand
Where white waves flashed on the shining sand!

Nearer and nearer it dashed, then lay
Like a fair white swan in the sheltered bay;
And Ronald leaped out, with a bound so free—
With bonnet and plume!—Oh, glad was she
As he sprung to her side and clasped to his heart
His Helen—" Dear Helen, no more we part."
   1863.

TO MARY MAIDEN.

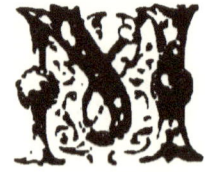AIDEN Mary, while I write,
Maiden art thou, blushing bright
As rosy dawn, and pure as light!

From orchards clouds of incense rise—
From opening flowers, whose liquid eyes
Look lovingly on friendly skies.

Music and odours fill thy room,
From birds that sing and violets' bloom,
And steep thy senses in perfume:

Above—below—yea, every sod
Of teeming earth,—the worm's damp clod,—
Pulse conscious of a present God.

TO MARY—MAIDEN.

Love's budding spring hath o'er thee past,
Summer blossoms rare thou hast,
Harvest hopes will gather fast.

Life to thee hath been a dream
Of dear delights—adown its stream
Thou'st floated full of joy supreme,

Adown life's current calm and clear,
Widening, deepening year by year,
Now thou'rt safely anchored here.

Hopeful, trustful on the shore
Of life's vast ocean; evermore
Hearing the surging billows roar.

Where treacherous wheels the eddying wave,
Which gulfs alike the vain, the brave,
Pleasure's votary, passion's slave.

But fear not, Mary; trust thy guide,
Trust the stout arm by thy side
To stem for thee life's fiercest tide.

TO MARY—WIFE.

MAIDEN Mary now hath flown,
Maidenhood to wifehood's given;
Matron Mary comes anon.

Launched on wedlock's rocky sea,
Duties new will come to thee;
Let clear-eyed faith thy pole-star be.

Though ills may fall, and densely shroud
Thy fairest hopes; with faith endowed,
Love beams the brighter for the cloud;

While earnest truth controls thy barque,
'Twill safely glide—love's favoured ark—
To shore of light, through tempests dark.

Remember, though awhile we tread
The dusty garden of the dead,
Eternal love shines overhead.

What though a speck be in the leaf,
Yield not thy soul to unbelief;
Love's doubting is the grief of grief!

No work is perfect: every flaw
That dims thy gem should tend to draw
Thy heart up to the higher law.

Trust on! Where faith is at the root
True love will blossom, branch, and shoot;
Guard well the flower: enjoy the fruit!

God bless thee in thy new estate!
May young affections ever wait
On thee, and thy heart's chosen mate!

THE FISHER-BOY'S VISION.

SUGGESTED BY LOUGH'S CHARMING MARBLE FIGURE.

HE fisher-boy rose in the morning grey,
   And let out his net in the calm, cool sea;
   He fished and he fished through the livelong day,
  But never a fish in sooth caught he.
He fished when the sun rose over the main,
  Shooting arrowy glances along the sea;
He patiently fished till it set again,
  Yet never a fish in his net caught he.

As musing he sat in his gliding boat,
  And silently looked on the glistening wave,
He caught the bold spirit of daring thought,
  The bravest companion a man can have.

A legion of happiest fancies met
    To gladden the fisher-boy far at sea;
When sudden a quivering stirred his net—
    "I have caught her at last, in sooth," thought he.

With throbbing of heart, and lips apart,
    He slowly lifted his net; and there,
In meshes of twine, lay a form divine,
    A beautiful being with golden hair!
The spirit-fed boy sprang up with joy,
    And clasped to his bosom—the vacant air!
The vision had flown, and he gazed alone—
    Alone on the moonlight streaming there.

1869.

MY LADY LOVE.

THE roses from the dewy briar were scattered one by one,
    The falling leaves came rustling from the high beech tree,
        As by the sleepy stream I wandered weary and alone,
    And thought upon my lady-love beyond the sea.
I thought of happy summer time when leaves were young and green,
    Of balmy blissful evenings and the trysting-tree,
Where a pressure of the palm and a smile of love serene,
    And a dainty cherry lip gave a heart to me.

The young trees, then so beautiful, are leafless, thin, and old :
    The merry music of the woods has now a wailing tone ;
The stream that glistened in the sun looks comfortless and cold,
    Oh, everything is altered since my lady-love is gone !

I listen for a laughing voice that never greets my
        ear,
    And for a lovely form I look that will not come
        to me;
Nor music, nor society, my troubled soul can
        cheer,
    They but swell the tide of sorrow in my heart's
        deep sea.

That rivers when they mingle, and their streams
        are lost in one,
    Should symbolize our future, was our dream
        of life: our pride!
But the current of our destiny divergingly must
        run,
    Resembling in its waywardness the rivers
        Tweed and Clyde.
One mountain range gives life to both, yet East
        and West they run,
    So East and West, for ever more, divided we
        must be.
And yet 'tis sweet to meditate, and know the
        joyous sun,
    Has cheered my darling's heart before it comes
        to gladden me.

Oh, I will ever love the sun, by morning, noon,
        and night.
    At morning, as a messenger her love he seems
        to bear;
At noon, because he perfecteth all being with his
        light;
    And at night because he carries her my blessing
        and my prayer.

Long as the sun shall, shining, bliss and wealth to mortals bring,
  My doting heart in faithfulness shall, sunlike, constant be;
And while it beats, in harmony my muse shall try to sing
  The praises of my lady-love far, far beyond the sea.

1855.

THE TIME TO MARRY.

HE would-be wise this counsel give,—
  "Let love's fond passion cool!
The man who early weds will live
  To think himself a fool.
  The galling chain that frets his limb
Wears deeper day by day,
Experience little teaches him
  Who gives the heart its way.
He wisely weds who weddeth late
A thrifty, unimpassioned mate."

When wrinkled oaks shall twining cling
  With tendrils like the vine;
When ravens like the linnet sing
  With melody divine;
When honey drops from withered leaves,
  And not from summer flowers;

When winter brings us golden sheaves,
　　And snow-drift sunny hours;
When truth abused makes falsehood right,
Go withering wed and find delight.

The trembling notes young birds awake
　　Rise sweetly into tune,
As April buds expanding make
　　The flowery wreath of June;
So love begun in life's young day
　　Matures with manhood's prime,
Defies the canker of decay,
　　And stronger grows with time;
O early quaff love's nuptial wine,
And all that's best in life is thine.

HOME LOVE.

I WILL not wander from the vale
    Across the heath so drear:
A charm abides within the vale,
    And makes me linger here.
'Tis not because the blackbirds fling
    Their love from tree to tree:
No, no! more sweet than birds can sing
    Is my wife's song to me!
    I will not wander from the vale,
        Nor cross the heath so drear;
    Love's sweet enchantment fills the vale,
        In love I'll linger here!

Blest vale, where in her cosy bower
    Sits nestling like a dove
My gentle mate; whose words create
    An atmosphere of love!
An atmosphere of holy love,
    Where sense and goodness dwell;
True love doth everything but love
    Instinctively repel.
    I will not wander from the vale,
        Nor cross the heath so drear;
    Love's sweet enchantment fills the vale,
        So I will linger here.

1848.

TO WHOM WE BOW.

WE will not bow to pomp or power,
　　Though crowned and seated high;
　　If truth be trodden under foot,
　　Such power we will defy!
But, oh, if justice, firm and mild,
　　With mercy tempered be,
We'll curb the passion running wild,
　　And willing bend the knee.

To hoarded wealth we will not bow,
　　Nor to its pampered lord;
Though dainties rare and perfumed air
　　Make magical his board.
But if his store he'll freely pour,
　　To lessen misery,
With loud acclaim, we hail the name,
　　And willing bend the knee!

The blooming thorn, the waving corn,
　　With ripened glory spread,
In grateful guise to dewy skies
　　And sunshine bend the head;

The lesson taught, with wisdom fraught,
   Shall unforgotten be;
With reverent brow to truth we bow,
   And grateful bend the knee.

1853.

PITY ME!

PITY me, pity me, ladies beautiful,
   Life is a wearisome load, I trow,
Pity me, pity me, young ones dutiful,
   Sorrow will furrow the fairest brow.
Out of the earth spring trees of beauty,
   Out of the tree come blossom and seed,
Out of the heart rise thoughts of duty,
   Ripening into word and deed;
Out of the purest, noblest natures,
   Weakling branches often spring,
All at the best are dependent creatures,
   Misery waileth while I sing.
      Pity me, pity me, ladies beautiful,
         Life is a wearisome load, I trow;
      Pity me, pity me, young ones dutiful,
         Sorrow will wrinkle the smoothest brow.

Pity me, pity me, ladies beautiful,
   Flowers will wither, though fair they seem;
Pity me, pity me, loving and dutiful,
   Life is not always a golden dream.

When I was young, upon me tended
    All that was loving, and true, and kind;
By the worthy and wise befriended,
    Nothing I needed I could not find.
He whose duty had been to cherish,
    False and felonious proved one day;
A desolate wintry leaf, I perish,
    Oh, save me from being a castaway!
        Pity me, pity me, ladies dutiful,
            Flowers will wither, though fair they seem:
        Pity me, pity me, ladies dutiful,
            Oh that my life had been all a dream!

1858.

MUSINGS IN MAY, 1875.

A SKETCH FROM NATURE.

BEHIND the hills the sun had set,
The grey clouds and the rosy met—
Embraced—their radiance lingers yet.

Fond wooers lingered in the glade,
As o'er them fell the evening shade:
Saluted—happy youth and maid!

Then followed whispers soft and low,
Confidings sweet, an overflow
Of tenderness, so dear to know.

Across the plain from far away,
Came music from a band at play—
A solemn requiem for the day;

Commingling came the singing breeze,
That harped among the chestnut trees,
Like murmurs from a hive of bees.

Then all was still. The stars awoke
And glimmered through the branching oak;
In fancy to myself I spoke:

MUSINGS IN MAY, 1875.

Would striving men a lesson learn
From Nature, soon would they discern
How poor the prize for which they yearn:

Oh what ambition, wealth, and power,
For which they peace and health devour,
Compared with this serenest hour!

The calm, o'erwhelming, filled my brain,
When screamed the fast approaching train
To whirl me back to town again!

And ever since, when troubles kill
My slumber, soon my heart I still,
When I recall that lonely hill;

That broomy hill on which I stood,
In pensive, calm, reflective mood,
Which brought my soul a world of good.

I meditate with joy intense,
Subdue each throbbing fevered sense,
And calmly wait my summons hence!

1875.

BESSIE HAS COME.

HAT shall we say
  Of the light of day?
    How shall we sing of the stars
      of night?
  What of the face
Whose beauty and grace
  So pleasantly shines, and makes blackness
    bright?

The snow may fall,
And spread like a pall
  Of virgin white on the gay green earth;
Dense fogs may loom
And make dark our room,
  Within it are voicings of joy and mirth.

From beautiful France,
Where sun rays glance,
  A stray beam comes to our wintry home,
To lessen the chill
Of our hearts, and fill
  Them with laughter and lovingness—BESSIE
    has come.
  1875.

THE TRANCE.

DESCRIBED AS SEEN.

THE fiery furnace ceased to glow,
The breathing bellows ceased to blow,
The clanging hammers ceased to ring.
We now could hear the skylark sing!
Instead of smoke wreaths curling high,
Were fleecy clouds—an azure sky,
O'er woody hills and grassy plains
Serene, the Sabbath stillness reigns.

By gentle slopes and forest trees
Came trooping down, in twos and threes,
Young maidens linking arm in arm,
Through shady lanes, by field and farm,
To where the humble chapel spread
Its table with memorial bread,
Where joyfully their voice they raise,
In words of prayer and songs of praise.

The preacher spoke with wondrous skill,
Till tender tears all eyelids fill;
When with the benediction given,
Each longing soul felt nearer heaven.

THE TRANCE.

The music hushed—the service o'er,
And all had gone save three or four,
Whilst one, so loving and beloved,
Still sat unmoving and unmoved.

A minute since she led the hymn,
To which the choiring seraphim
Entranced might listen, filled with love,
To bear the cadence sweet above:
A moment since her eyes were bright,
And now they shrouded are as night,
Her lips are closed, her tongue is tied,
Her hands fall feebly by her side.

"Oh misery!" "Not so, not so,"
A gentle voice spake soft and low,
"We know the cause, we also know
'Tis but a trance that soon will go."
The paling lips, the cheeks, the brow,
Were bathed with water cool, and now
Her colour came; with sounding sighs
She opened wide her wondering eyes.

"Where am I? Oh, where have I been?
Such sounds I've heard, such sights I've seen!
Where am I? Oh, where am I? Speak!
Quick, quick, or else my heart will break.
Oh now I know! It was the hymn
That called me to my Saviour! Him
I've seen, and would with Him remain.
Why did you bring me back again?"

"Have patience, dearest—oh, be still,
"Be calm!" "'Tis hard, but oh I will!

THE TRANCE.

Again I hear my Saviour's call!
I come! I come! my life, my all.
Oh Jesus, Saviour, Thou art mine!
Oh answer, Jesus, am I Thine?"
Once more arose the wild refrain,
" Why did you bring me back again?"

Soon peaceful as a child at rest,
She sat, her palms crossed on her breast,
A brief space more, and then her eyes
Were opened with a meek surprise.
" My children! Oh, my husband!—Come,
Now I am happy!—Take me home.
I've been in heaven—I saw it plain,
I'm glad you called me back again."

In painless weakness long she lay,
Illusions led her mind astray.
But strength returned, and when at last
She woke to reason, all the past
Was as a dream, that leaves behind
The vaguest impress on the mind;
Serenely now to health restored,
She lives to thank and praise her Lord.

1875.

GARPEL GLEN—A MEMORY.[1]

REMEMBER? How well I remember the day,
When cousinly kindliness pointed the way
    To lonely Glen Garpel, whose stream is a theme
For manhood to muse on, and maidens to dream;
Where nature and art are so blended in one,
That 'tis hard to discover where art has begun.

The trees of the forest—the white blooming thorn,
These green in their leafage—that sweet in the morn—

---

[1] These few lines were sketched from memory after visiting the Glen. They very faintly express the intense pleasure I felt on the occasion. The day was charming, and as the mist rolled away, the upper part of the Glen unfolded its exquisite loveliness. But its great natural curiosity is the alum rock, which, although a piece of it when placed in the mouth yields no taste, still, when water is dashed on its face, and gathered as it trickles down the channels on its cheek, it contains a strong solution of alum.

The trout in the streamlet—the foam on the
  pool—
The cloven rock rising so shady and cool:
Had all passed unheeded, unnoted by me,
But for one whose love led me their beauties to see.

On the soft mossy mound for a while we reposed,
Whilst nature her beauties but dimly disclosed;
The bracken-hid fountain, so close to the waste,—
So small to the vision, so sweet to the taste:
Its tiny drops trickling, delightful to sip,
Seemed only to waken new thirst on the lip.

There's a tongue in the sunbeam, a voice in the
  breeze,
Whilst tremulous whispers creep under the trees,
With thrillings of rapture like stingings of pain,
Or passionate longings for cool falling rain—
There, tuned to the notes of the sweet-cooing
  dove,
Walk, hand in hand, wooers who whisper their
  love.

Ascending—descending the rustic-built stair,
We gathered lush strawberries, rosy and rare,
Whilst earth-blossoms, bruised by our feet on the
  sod,
Raised odours appealing for care how we trod!
So tender hearts crushed may a spirit reveal
As touching as blossoms when bruised by the heel.

I watched the "wee burnie," its windings and
  falls,
Its curvings fantastic round steep rocky walls—

Now hid for a moment—emerging again
It glancingly danced to the stream in the plain.
Ah me! Now environed by millions of men,
I long to revisit Glen Garpel again!

   May, 1873.

THE EAST.

THE East, the East, the beautiful East!
  Whence issued all life in the light of day;
    Where starlit skies
    Led on the Wise
  To worship the God as He cradled lay!

The East, the East, the bountiful East!
  Where liberty, learning, and art arose;
    Where honour and faith
    Wrought havoc and scaith,
  And a handful triumphed o'er countless foes.

The East, the East, the intolerant East!
  Where men like chattels were bought and sold,
    Where iron and stone
    Ground muscle and bone,
  Condemned of Heaven for thirst of gold!

The East, the East, the blasphemous East!
  Whence honour, and virtue, and truth are driven;
    Where frenzied hordes,
    With profaning words,
  Bestow on a tyrant the dues of Heaven.

The East, the East, the detestable East!
  Corrupt and polluted with vilest sin;
    In city and glen,
    'Mongst women and men,
  The rottenest hearts have the smoothest skin.

The East, the East, the degenerate East!
  Barbarians revel where angels dwelt,
    They quake with fear,
    For their end is near,
  And their glory, like snow in the sun, will melt.

The East, the East, the afflicted East!
  Where dauntless masses destroying meet;
    The gallantest forms
    Are laid with worms,
  And the drifted snow is their winding-sheet.

The East, the East, the distracted East!
  Where kindred peoples are armed as foes!
    The crystalline flood
    Runs red with blood,
  And curses are falling where blessings arose.

The East, the East, there is hope for the East!
  The Tyrant[1] is struck in his gilded room;
    Gaunt figures arise,
     With flaming eyes,
And beckon the despot to meet his doom.

The East, the East, the uplifted East!
  With millions rejoicing in fruitful vales;
    The troubles are stilled,
    And the earth is filled
With the hum of a people where peace prevails.

---

[1] These verses were written during the Crimean War, and printed fourteen days before the reported death of the Emperor Nicholas.

THE DIGNITY OF LABOUR.

A SONG FOR THE NEWLY-ENFRANCHISED.
DEDICATED TO WORKERS, BY A WORKER.

ALL ye who would enfranchised be,
    Let passion yield to reason:
The worker, worthy to be free,
    Abhorreth blood and treason.
    Remembering who and what we are,
The glorious time before us,
Preferring peace to thirsty war,
    Your voices raise in chorus—
      The time has come for man to love
      All people as his neighbour;
      The time has come for us to prove
      The dignity of labour.

Five hundred years of toil and strife,
    With hearts and souls undaunted,
We've fought for Liberty; and now
    Secured the rights we wanted.
The truly noble—wise and good,
    Shall yet rejoice to see, men,

How little we've been understood,
  How great we are as free-men.
    The time has come for man to love
      The nations as his neighbour;
    The time has come for us to prove
      The dignity of labour.

We make the swamp a fruitful field,
  The desert wild a garden,—
To kindly words our feelings yield,
  Distrust our spirits harden.
By head and hand rule sea and land
  With power condensed and fervent,—
The flood and flame we boldly tame,
  And lightning make our servant.
    The time has come for man to love
      All nations as his neighbour;
    The time has come for us to prove
      The dignity of labour.

We feel, and can control our strength,
  And will, with faith unswerving,
Protect our own, yet yield to all
  The rights they are deserving—
The right to think, the right to work
  With whom and how he pleases;
The law that fetters thought and skill
  The honest spirit teases.
    The time has come for man to love
      All nations as his neighbour;
    The time has come for us to prove
      The dignity of labour.

We well can judge 'twixt sound and sense,
  The true from false distinguish,

Reject mere brawling eloquence,
  And self-conceit extinguish;
But self-respect—the word direct,
  The modest, manly bearing—
Is prized as giving truth a grace,
  And worth a noble daring.
    The time has come for man to love
      All nations as his neighbour;
    The time has come for us to prove
      The dignity of labour.

The men we choose will ne'er abuse
  The privilege we lend them,
But face the storm, and well perform
  The work to which we send them;
To right the wrong—in right be strong,
  Despising grosser leaven;
To scorn the bribe, in truth abide,
  And leave the rest to Heaven.
    Too long, too long we've subject been
      To power—and pelf, its neighbour;
    The time has come for us to prove
      The dignity of labour.

ELECTED! Plead our holy cause
  In each distinct relation,
Yet gently touch those ancient laws,
  The bulwarks of the nation;
Maintain supreme the Parliament,
  Oppressive wrongs redress, men;
Remember what you represent,
  And God your efforts bless, men.
    The time has come for man to love
      All people as his neighbour;
    The time has come, and we will prove
      The dignity of labour.

POLISH EXILE'S DREAM.

WHILST I, a homeless exile, slept
    In far Siberia's frigid clime,
I had a dream, a glorious dream,
    That may be true in future time.

Methought I heard a murmuring hum
    Of voices, like the distant sea;
And then ten thousand tongues, as one,
    Proclaimed, "REDEMPTION! POLAND'S FREE!"

I listened; loud, and louder still.
    The strain fell on my greedy ear:
"Arise, brave men, your homes are free!
    Your homes to love and honour dear!"

The despot stood within our power:
    With stern rebuke we bade him go
And think upon his ruthless deeds
    As punishment!—an endless woe!

I saw the bauble crown cast down,
    I saw the jewelled sceptre broke,
Our chains fall off!—then with a gush
    Of holiest feeling, I awoke!

Oh sad reverse! My limbs were chained
   Within a gloomy dungeon drear;
I raised my voice—'twas all in vain,
   No sympathizing soul was near!

My dizzy brain was all in flame,
   My blood rushed through it like a stream
Of liquid fire. Kind Heaven decree
   That this may not be all a dream.

I pray, that yet before I die,
   Our land's deliverance I may see;
And hail with all a patriot's soul
   The heaven-born star of liberty!

    1836.

SHE CAME AMONG US.

SHE came among us full of life,
    Whoever saw her blest her;
Nor joyous maid nor happy wife
    But loved her as a sister.
A ringing music swelled her voice,
    So full of light and laughter;
Remembrance made the heart rejoice
    In rapture ever after.

No special lustre filled the eye,
    Or spread her cheek with blossom;
But goodness freighted every sigh
    That heaved her gentle bosom.
When she was near, we never thought
    How much of love we owed her;
Now she is gone, remorse is wrought
    So little love we showed her.

The genial mirth that cheered our hearth,
    To which we loved to hearken,
Is gone, and where its presence shone
    Deep falling shadows darken!

O'er every brow a gloom is spread,
   On every heart a sadness,
Bright memories filling heart and head,
   More distant keep our gladness!

As light when lost is prized the most,
   Speed night and welcome morrow;
Our message wing, and quickly bring
   Her back to banish sorrow!
Why she's so dear, when she is near,
   Perchance we may discover;
Words may express her lovingness,
   But not how much we love her.

1852.

I CANNA BE FASHED.[1]

"I CANNA be fashed!" was the sullen reply
    Of my mother, one day. How deep was the sigh
    Of my father, meek man!—nae word did he speak
As he turned, and a tear trembled over his cheek;
'Twas the bane of my life; I had better been thrashed
Than have heard the sharp answer—"I canna be fashed."

It twisted my temper—it hardened my will—
The good I attempted would ever come ill;
A plague to all households—a breeder o' strife;
Opposition and idleness grew wi' my life;
Advice was unheeded—wi' brow unabashed,
My answer was ever—"I canna be fashed."

Idle and ignorant, fretful and vain;
I grew up to womanhood—not very plain:

---

[1] Cannot be "troubled," or, in the language of excitement, "bothered."

Could dance—was attractive—but quickly the yoke
Of my charms became powerless whenever I spoke.
Every nerve of my heart was with agony lashed,
And I sorely repented, "I canna be fashed."

I still had admirers who'd flatter and sue,
They were vain as myself, and as ignorant too:
They buzzed and they fluttered like moths round the light—
Beginning with wrong—the wrong never came right.
So hope was extinguished, and charity crashed,
For to win or deserve them "I couldna be fashed."

And now at the age of some thirty and nine,
How few are the conquests I reckon as mine:
Unloved and unloving, how woefu' my lot,
With cup and with kitten alone in my cot;
My goblet of joy in a moment was dashed
From my lips by a withering "canna be fashed."

My lesson, dear sisters—pray learn it while young—
The worst ill o' life is a bridleless tongue.
All pride is a pest! and the arrow of wit,
When pointed with passion, is ever unfit
For a womanly tongue; but if kindness be flashed,
Continue it—say not "I canna be fashed."

1854.

THE MAIDEN'S FRIEND.

A WEE bird frae its leafy spray
    Sang, "Lassie, wake, awake!
      The lad you loe,
      Sae leal an' true,
    Is sighing for your sake!"
I quickly rose, slipped on my clothes,
    An' neath the hawthorn tree,
      The lad I loe,
      Sae leal an' true,
    I found awaiting me.

The simmer sun rose o'er the hill,
    The laverock whistled clear,
      Around our feet
      The clover sweet
    Shed fragrance sweet an' dear;
But sweeter far than blossoms are
    Were Willie's words to me;
      An' him I'll loe,
      Sae leal an' true,
    Until the day I dee.

Again, again the birdie sings
  Amang the blooming boughs!
    It seemed to hear,
    It sang to cheer
  Our lipping plighting vows;
Oh, ever sing wi' raptured wing,
  My birdie in the tree;
    The lad I loe
    Sae leal an' true
  Is health an' wealth to me!

1870.

WOOING AND WEDDING.

YOUNG Andrew lived by Craigie
    burn,
  An' Jessie bloomed by Moffat
    Water,
  He a laird sae blythe an' free,
An' she a shepherd's winsome daughter.
    Oh, their lives were bright and cheery,
    Nothing came to make them e'erie;
    Well he knew she was his deary,
    She o' him was never weary.

Through the rocky woody glens,
  Owre the hills sae green an' grassy,
Wooing wandered, arm in arm,
  Happy, happy lad an' lassie.
    Oh, their lives were bright an' cheery,
    Nothing came to make them e'erie;
    Well he knew she was his deary,
    She o' him was never weary.

By the Grey Mare's feathery fu',
  By the lonesome Loch o' Lowes,
At Saint Mary's holy shrine
  Pledged they solemn, sacred vows!

Oh, their lives were bright an' cheery,
Nothing came to make them e'erie;
Well he knew she was his deary,
She o' him was never weary.

Oh dool upon it! dreadful war,
  Ghastly scars an' strife an' slaughter!
Andrew pressed!—maun fight afar,
  Jessie weeps by Moffat Water!
Now her days were sad an' dreary,
Naething left to make her cheery;
Oh, the nights were lang an' e'erie,
She o' life itself was weary.

Darkest hour is nearest dawn;
  Joy may watch by sorrow sleeping;
Rainbow arches beaming bright,
  Only show when clouds are weeping.
Jessie's days were sad an' dreary,
Naething left to make her cheery;
Oh, the nights were long an' e'erie,
She o' life itself was weary.

But war will cease, an' men return!
  A captain came to Moffat Water!
An' proudly bore to Craigie burn,
  As wedded wife, the shepherd's daughter!
Never mair the days were dreary;
Never mair the nights were e'erie;
Night an' day for ever cheery;
They o' love will never weary,
Never, never, never weary.

"I WILL TRY."[1]

"I WILL try, I will try," was the answer I gave
    To my Mentor in youth, who engaged to dispel
The darkness o'erclouding my brain; for, in sooth,
I found nothing so hard as to figure and spell.
Bewildered and bothered, my only reply
Was, "I feel it is hard, but I'll try, sir, I'll try."

By trying, some knowledge I think was enshrined;
    At least, my companions would upwardly look
With eyes so imploring, I seldom declined
    To help to unravel some problem or book:
Though frequently puzzled, I'd gently reply,
"I think it is hard, but I'll try, lad, I'll try."

And then came the time when new feelings awoke,
    And I timidly shrank from the glance of an eye,

---

[1] "'I will try' is one of the truest principles, and expresses all that one man has any right to expect from another. I think I shall adopt it as a motto."—NATHANIEL HAWTHORNE.

Yet courage might come when the silence was
    broke,—
    I stammered, but lost all my voice in a sigh.
Then courage, my heart!—why silent, oh why?
Speak boldly your meaning—I'll try, I must try!

I ventured, I conquered, and ever since then
    No danger e'er daunted my spirit or will;
Commanded to rush with a handful of men
    Through the breach, in the teeth of the blazing
        guns—still
To the test, "Are you able?" I'd calmly reply,
"The duty is hard, but I'll try, sir, I'll try."

And now when the battle of life has been won,
    And I garrulous speak of my deeds in the past;
Though I sit in the shade, I look up at the Sun,
    And hope for one victory more—'tis the last.
'Tis scaling those ramparts, far up in the sky!
Art able? In faith, I will try, I will try!

SONNETS.

"In sounding sonnets Poets may embalm
　The ever-changing passions of the hour;
　Love, Hatred, Friendship, evermore should pour
Like us a river, turbulent or calm.
　But greatest he, whose wide-embracing dower
Of thought is filled with Truth, and holy as a Psalm."

From Provençal Sonnets.

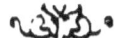

HOWARD.

THERE is a manly music in the name
    Of Howard, that demands the skill
    Of Milton's measure, all our hearts
        to thrill
    Whilst voicing his imperishable fame,
As with a trumpet, which immortals hear,
And back to mortals echo it again,
In praise of him who broke the captive's chain;
    Before whose radiant face the atmosphere
Of dungeons deadly dank was purified,—
    As if the sun had left his heavenly sphere
And sought the cells where helpless thousands
        died,—
    Gaunt Death, o'ergorged, before him fled in
        fear:
And, like a vulture cheated of its prey,
Spread wide his sable wings, and, scowling, soared
        away.

1840.

TO WORDSWORTH.

GREAT Poet, Wordsworth!—ho-
noured and admired,—
O tell me how my soul can best
express
Its adoration of a bard inspired,—
A bard all wisdom, love, and gentleness!
No fiery passions in thy bosom rage,
No thoughts malignant in thy works are seen;
Fair Nature's self looks forth from every page,
The poet's only guide to fame, I ween:
Exalting virtue, purifying man,
Has been thy task, and nobly is it done!
May Heaven prosper what thy wishes plan,
And grant long life to wear thy fame well won;
Mayst thou on death, when death o'ercometh life,
Smile like a bridegroom on his new-made wife!

1838.

TO HAYDON.

ON SEEING HIS PAINTING OF CHRIST'S TRIUMPHAL ENTRY INTO JERUSALEM.

HAT great magician of the earth art thou,
  Who hast such wonders on the canvas wrought?
    In rapt astonishment I gaze, for now
Those hearts seem bursting with excess of thought;
Another touch,—those forms will move and speak,
  Proclaiming to the world their author's name,
On whom Sir Sycophant may vengeance wreak,
  But cannot pluck a tittle from his fame!
Wherever art or schools of art may be,
  His name with theirs is bound incorporate;
And they shall live when that monopoly,
  A nation's shame, lies waste and desolate.
Art's brightest stars thy works will ever shine—
The Hebrew "Triumph," Haydon, shall be thine!

NAPOLEONIC.

1.

BESIDE the lighthouse of Antibes I stand,
   And gazing seaward, faintly can discern
   The Isle of Corsica;—from which we learn
Great men may grow on smallest specks of land:
From that lone spot, that rocky, rugged strand,
   Napoleon came, imperious and stern,
The scourge of peoples and the dread of kings,
He dealt out vengeance with unsparing hand;
   Yet, as the storm bears healing on its wings,
   So he, unthinking, lifted meaner things,—
Poor puny souls,—to think and act like men;
   Whilst he, their idol, was the first to fall:
O righteous sacrifice! Not knowing when
   To stop, he strove to bind, and found himself in thrall.

NAPOLEONIC.

II.

NOW turning westward.   There the placid bay
   That gleams between me and Saint
      Marguerite,
   Where long in chains the iron-
masked victim lay!
Here! dappled waters lave the pilgrim's feet!
Beyond is Cannes, where sparkling mansions rise,
   And folks from every nation congregate—
Poet and painter—ignorant and wise—
   Men of renown lay by their robes of state!
A motley group in sooth—cohesion none!
   There, nearer, straggling on the coral sand,
The sleepy Jouan basketh in the sun!
   Napoleon, 'scaped from Elba, there did land
To set all Europe in a second flame;
And gave to Jouan's Gulf both history and fame.

    ANTIBES, *Jan.* 1867.

TO GARIBALDI.[1]

I.

MUSING stood upon the beach at Nice!
  Behind — unseen — the thoughtless world passed by;
  Before—the ocean, bluer than the sky,
    Its great breast heaved, and laved the shore in peace.
I thought of him—the Patriot—whose increase
  Of greatness, spreads wide circling as the foam,
  In grateful murmurs. This his early home!
His home no more, nor country—sad release—
  Strange mutability! A 'stablish'd throne!—
  Italia free! His birthplace,—birthright gone!
Men blame his king, and mourn the sad mischance.
That linked fair Nice to greedy, grasping France.

---

[1] Written within view of the house reputed to have been the home of the great General, and probably the place in which he was born. It is the middle one of three, standing at the head of the harbour of Nice, and easily recognized by its being a story lower than the other two. From the one to the eastward was flapping the tricolor of France.

Yet grieve not, Garibaldi—Freedom's sun will shine,
And link immortally Italia's fame to thine!

TO GARIBALDI.[1]

II.

HERE! on that height, I played when yet a child,
  And gazed with rapture on the wide-spread sea,
  My young heart throbbing—planning things to be.
My country was a byword, and reviled:
  The hydra tyrant crushed it. To be free
Men bravely strove, but dreamily and wild!
Now, now 'tis done—Italia reconciled!
  One glorious people, one most loyal king!
Yet here in tears I linger—there the place
Where first I saw the light, heartsore I trace
  In hateful hues, a strange flag fluttering!
  What some call policy—I call disgrace,
And plunge my hands in the inviolate sea!
For thus I wash my soul, detested France, of thee!

ANTIBES, *Jan.* 1867.

---

[1] The second sonnet refers to the report that after the transfer of Nice to France Garibaldi visited his native place in disguise, and in deep grief felt himself homeless, and bade farewell to Nice for ever.

TO MAJOR JAMES WALTER.

ON MÜLLER'S PICTURE,
"THE READING OF DANTE."

MÜLLER, thy paintings to my soul reveal
   A thrilling gladness; as when old friends meet,
   Clasped palm in palm they feel their strong hearts beat
In unison—so I to Nature kneel
Whilst gazing on thy picture; for I feel
   Each graceful line—each thoughtful touch and tone
   Of rare affection, purifies mine own;
Thus earthly love's refined by one ideal.
Within this gentle lady's trustful eyes
   The poet's story has divinely wrought,
Till from their dovelike orbs out-beam surprise.
   And new-born rapture with her new-born thought;

With mind matured, well pleased, her chosen
    guide,
Through Dante's deathless page leads lovingly his
    bride.

ON BOARD THE "NIAGARA" STEAMSHIP,
    August, 1848.

PROMISES.

BUT little faith in promises! for men
    Who freely promise, seldom well
        perform;
    And willingly forget thee when the
        storm
Approaches darkly;—but, return again
When genial sunshine animates the plain
    Of thy torn heart: and patronizing talk
Of thy reverses—how they suffered pain
    Intensest for thy sake.—The feeble stalk
Of a frail reed is stronger staff, than friend
    Like this to lean on: weathercock to wheel
With every breeze, but stretch no helping hand:
    Incarnate selfishness from head to heel.
I've suffered much, and suffering this have learned
The true man works in silence, where his friend's
    concerned.

    1858.

APRIL SONNET.

No. I.

APRIL KIND.

APRIL, though treacherous and
    changeling named,
    Wanton and wayward in thy
    nature, still
    Revealest thou those mysteries
that fill
All hearts with love's deep sympathy, and famed
    For blooms that odorous balm distil.
Birthtime of beauty and of poesy:
    When birds betrothed melodious from the hill
Rain down their morning song of ecstasy.
    When amorous bees toy fondly with the
    flower,
And drain its humid sweets deliriously,
    Faint with excess, in love's delicious bower
Softly infolded, blossom-couched he lies:
Whilst draughts of fragrant dew oblivious sleep
    supplies.

April, 1855.

APRIL SONNET.

No. II.

APRIL CRUEL.

APRIL, ah me! how swiftly changes come,
   How soon the month we love we learn to hate,
   When boughs deflowered hang down disconsolate,
And clouds of grief make dark our garden home,
   Where genial sunshine lingering loved to wait;
With joy we grafted in thy wounded rind
   The fairest branch that ever blossom bore;
Clasped close, incorporate as one combined,
   A newborn rapture trembled in thy core
   As budding life expanded, more and more
We longed to reap the fruit; but woke to find
   Hope in a morning blighted; from the shore
A ruthless wind stole with untimely frost,
And all thy cherished bloom was shrivelled, loosed, and lost.

April, 1855.

SUGGESTED BY LOUGH'S "ARIEL."

I.—THE SCULPTOR TO THE SPIRIT.

STAY! O stay, thou wondrous spirit, stay!
　Vouchsafe a while to glad my raptured sight,
　　Nor speed thee on so quickly in thy flight;
Rein in thy steed, which loves the twilight grey,
　Flitting for ever 'twixt the day and night.
Impulsive fluttering with thy restless wings—
　Wheeling impetuous in the wake of light,
Till darkness o'er the earth her mantle flings.
　What art thou, spirit, in thy true estate,
　That thou on earth should deign to scatter bliss?
　　Thou purest sprite that genius could create!
Thou rare embodiment of faithfulness!
Oh! I would sketch thy lineaments divine,
And every home in England make thy sacred shrine!

II.—To the Poet Sculptor.

WE thank thee, gentle Ariel, thou hast stayed
  Until each feature in thy form we trace
  In lines of beauty. Time shall not efface,
Though he, Iconoclastic, plies his trade!
Imagination's airy visions fade
  Or change. Depending upon words alone
Sad havoc with our choicest thoughts is played:
  They pass, we would recall them, they have flown!
Not so thy spirit, Ariel; it is here.
  Spreading a radiant atmosphere around!
The gazer's eye swims with a lustrous tear;—
  Entranced he stands:—The place is holy ground.
What Shakespeare's fancy glowingly portrayed,
The Poet Sculptor's skill hath here immortal made.

1858.

TO E. S. DALLAS.

IN sculptured stone, on stately columns raise
The graceful dome high lifted in the air,
In memory of the great whose merits rare
Draw forth a grateful people's honest praise:
While laureates hymn their deeds in sounding lays!
　Yet, pillar, arch, and dome shall crumble there,
The hero's name itself forgotten be:
　Dust unto dust, deriding human care.
Verse—verse alone gives immortality.
　True verse—true art—undying fame secures,
Whilst all beside may wither, fade and flee,
　A spark from heaven, like heaven itself endures,
True thought—true work—embalmed in art survive,
The glory of the dead—a joy to all alive!

　January, 1867.

TO J. G., ON HER WEDDING DAY.

DAUGHTER of him and her, of whom to be
   A friend is no small privilege: full orbed
   Their love abides, and cannot be absorbed
By those who would surround them with a sea
  Of flattery. Sharing their merit, thou,
  Clear in thy spirit, clear in heart and brow;
Clear in thy love, as thou wouldst have *one* be
Clear of all doubtings in his love for thee,—
  Clear be thy future as transparent now!
I would as one who holds in memory
  The vision of a bright and beautiful
  Young being, seldom sad, and never dull,
Utter a brief God bless thee! May thy life
Henceforth by love be guarded as a leal, brave wife.

August 10, 1874.

TO FREDERICK LATREILLE.

HERE is a sympathy that poets feel:
   There is a joy that only poets know;
A kindred gladness in a brother's weal,
   A kindred sadness in a brother's woe:
From them the tear compassionate doth flow
With mutual gushings, soothing their distress;
   Affection strong, that no reserve can bow,
Nor leave them in the world companionless!
Such are thy feelings, Fred'rick, for in thee
   Love, truth, and justice most benignly blend
With lofty purposes supremely free!
   Deep is the love I bear thee, worthy friend,
For friend thou art, in wintry hours no less
Than when life's summer smiles in rosiest loveliness!

1838.

"NYMPH AND GOAT."

PASTORAL GROUP IN MARBLE: J. G. LOUGH, SCULPTOR.

HAVE patience, mischief! whilst I wreathe your brow,
Your horns, your ears, your neck, as I do now,
With leaves unfading from immortal trees
That in Elysia grow: the gods to please!
Who knows but in the ages yet to be,
Struck with the pastoral loves of you and me,
Some genius guided sole by nature's rules,
Undwarfed by cramping teaching of the schools
May learn our friendship in the glades and groves,
And tell in art the story of our loves?
Just as we are, enraptured, all alone,
Grandly transfigured into breathing stone;
Placed high above the passions of the hind,
To charm for evermore intelligent mankind.

1875.

GIPSIES.

HOW sweet the stillness of the autumn wood,
How soft the cushion of the velvet moss,
On which recline the vagrant brotherhood
Of wandering gipsies—knowing not the loss
Of house or home, whilst curtained by the fern,
Roofed by the spreading branches of the trees,
Through whose quaint interlacing they discern
The broken radiance of the sun—or learn
The movements of the starry host by night,
And slumber softly sheltered from the breeze,
Hushed by the murmurs of the far off seas,
But promptly waking with the dawning light,
Begin the aimless loiter of their lives,
Untaxed they pilfer, feed, and swarm as bees in hives.

1874.

TO MRS. LOUGH.

ON THE MARRIAGE OF HER DAUGHTER "INA."

WHEN joy abounds, why falls the scalding tear?
Why heaves the breast with breath-suspending sighs?
When friends are gathered round to bid thee cheer,
And faith in love looks bright in INA's eyes,
And her fond husband's silent look replies,
Truly and proudly, "INA need not fear
Whilst my strong arm and sheltering love are near."
What has been must be, parents must resign
Their dearest idol to another's care.
Thy mother's pang, retributive is thine!
Who suffers love, must love's sweet sufferings bear,
And bear them joyously. 'Tis still decreed
The world is bright with flowers, where love and honour lead.

1853.

TO SIR JOHN AND LADY KEY.

ON THE ANNIVERSARY OF THEIR MARRIAGE.

THRICE seven years of ardent life had passed
    With all the eagerness of buoyant youth,
    Ripening to manhood; thirsting for the truth,
And loyalty and love of woman, cast
    In the mould of beauty. And soon in sooth
Thy cherished hopes were compassed, very fast
    Thy heart beat with its new triumph. Uncouth
And dread imaginings were cast aside;
Thy soul's fond idol stood thy blushing bride,
    And has for seasons more than I dare name
Thy consolation been; ever by thy side,
    To cheer thee with devotion's steady flame.
In calm prosperity thy joy and guide,
She changed not with the varying fickle tide
Of popular applause. Through storm and strife
She shone for evermore the blessing of thy life.

THORNBURY, 1853.

TO THE MEMORY OF JAMES LOCKE.

THE tolling bell sounds faintly from the hill,
   As winding slowly through the silent vale,
     The dark procession moves beneath a veil
Of dismal clouds, which gloomy thoughts instil,
And hearts bereaved with sacred sadness fill:
   The sable garb—the cheeks so ashy pale,
The eyes which shed no simulated tear,
   Express the deep emotions that prevail!
When friends are gone whose memories are dear,
Their forms familiar often reappear
   Mid scenes discordant; festive, blythe, or gay;
And with their presence fill the mental eye!
   'Tis thus, departed friend, thy name will stay
Deep graven on our hearts, it can but with us die.

BLACKHEATH.

WHENCE come those lofty strains of hymning praise,
   That chain instinctively the wandering ear?
Now faintly flowing—now melodious, clear,
In graceful modulations; like the lays
   Of earnest worshippers the Alps among;
Or those stern-hearted, God-befriended men,
Who for *the faith*, made Scotland, hill and glen,
   A temple vocal with divinest song—
   Unfaltering right curbing despotic wrong.
Even here, the lewd are stayed with solemn words.
Listen! that voice some precious truth affords:
   " Beware the tempter!—Be in Virtue strong!—
Wine cannot soothe—it bids fierce passion rage:
O nurse thine oil of youth to feed thy lamp of age!"

PÈRE LA CHAISE.

MOCK not the manner any one may
    choose
  To show respect to dear friends
    passed away;
  The pulsing heart must turn to
common clay,
But He who made it, never will refuse
  The offering of the soul devout, and may
Accept the custom, sanctify the use
  Of symbols offered on the shrine of death—
Mortal immortels fading every hour,
  And melting in the common air like breath.
  Though false the doctrine, they who hold the
    faith
Sincerely, working in its light with power,
  The HEAD SUPREME will judge 'twixt thou and
    them;
Whilst Charity, in softest accents, saith—
  "Judge gently, mortal man, lest thou thyself
    condemn!"

TO COMPANIONS IN TRAVEL, WITH THE POEMS OF LONGFELLOW.

IN vain, dear friends, for fitting phrase we seek
    To tell you all the gratitude we feel
    For many acts of kindness, hearty zeal.
  And truest sympathy. O words are weak,
And will not to ourselves our thoughts reveal;
Therefore, of friendship let the Poet speak—
  The high-souled Poet of the far-off West—
  Whose lofty language soars where eagles rest,
And gilds with glorious thought each Alpine peak:
Or falling, dewlike, on the verdant sward,
  His verse prolific pleasant thoughts suggest
O think and feel that then your friends are heard;
  And what to you seems worthiest, wisest, best;
  Is but what friendship feels, by pen inspired expressed.

DAUPHINY ALPS—GRAND CHARTREUSE.

YE marvellous cliffs—ye everlasting hills
   Pointing to heaven; like princely warders stand:
   Within your shade I reverently bend,
Where flowery bloom the air with fragrance fills;
And vales made musical by clamouring rills
   Swelling the torrent in its dark abyss;
Within whose depths the warm sun seldom shines
Through the dense foliage of mountain pines:
   Yet all around a Son has shone, I wis;
For here Saint BRUNO raised an altar throne,
   And left his mark unfadingly in this
Lone vale! By running streams, on jutting stone—
   On loftiest crag with coronet of moss,
   Is lifted high o'er all the ever sacred cross.

1865.

SACRED.

"Blessings be with them and eternal praise,
Who gave us nobler loves and nobler cares;
The poets, who on earth have made us heirs
Of Truth and pure delight, by heavenly lays."
                                                              WORDSWORTH.

THE LORD'S PRAYER.

OUR Father who in heaven art,
  Thy name for ever hallowed be;
Thy kingdom come—Thy will be done
  As 'tis in heaven—on earth and sea.

Give us each day our daily bread,
  And all our trespasses forgive;
As we forgive the trespassers,
  Who make it very hard to live.

Lord, guard us from temptation strong,
  And from all evil us deliver;
For Thine the power and kingdom is,
  And glory ever, and for ever!

1875.

HYMN ON FOUNDING A SCHOOL OR CHURCH.[1]

GOD of Life, at Whose command
The wondrous world from chaos came;
    Through countless years,
    The rolling spheres
Thy glory and Thy power proclaim.

O God of Love, when man rebelled,
And wildly wandered far from Thee,
    Thy heart did yearn
    For his return,
Repentant—pardoned—blest and free.

O God of Grace, though lost—corrupt
In word and work, in heart and brain,
    The streaming flood
    Of Jesu's blood
Has power to cleanse from every stain.

---

[1] From "Lyra Britannica."

With grateful hearts, O Lord, to Thee,
We would in earnest work engage:
    To teach Thy truth
    To wayward youth,
And consolation bring to age.

Do Thou, O God, our efforts bless,
To plant and spread Thy word divine
    By vale and hill,
    With all our skill!
And all the glory, Lord, be Thine.

1866.

A MORNING HYMN.

LL praise, my Father, be to Thee,
Who through the night hast guarded me,
And spread before my waking eyes
The grassy vales and azure skies.

I see Thy bounty in the plains,
Where lavish love in beauty reigns;
From far beyond the peaks of snow,
Thy living streams of mercy flow.

When weak with woe and sore oppressed,
How sweet to lay us down to rest,
In humble faith that Christ our Lord
Will lift the weight, or strength afford.

For weary months upon my bed
Thy care sustained my troubled head!
Assuaged the grief—allayed the pain
Of aching heart and restless brain.

As now far up the cloudless sky
The glorious sun ascends on high,
And sheds his beams upon the plain,
To swell the fruit and gild the grain:

So from Thy Son our Lord, whose home
Encircles all the starry dome,
Come rays of love in affluence given
To ripen souls for Him and Heaven.
    1873.

FOR HIGHER LIFE.

COME, Spirit of the living Lord,
    As come the summer breezes;
Revive in me the latent word,
    The WORD that ever pleases.

Come play around this stubborn heart,
    So chill within my bosom;
Destroy the hard, the icy part,
    And make it bud and blossom.

O make it bud with holy thought,
    And bloom in human kindness;
So ripening into deed, be brought
    To clear the soul from blindness:—

That blindness which on thoughtless youth
    Is ever close attendant;—
The film remove—make Love and Truth
    Be seen in the ascendant:

Ascending higher, higher still,
    By light of Gospel story;
Till earthly thoughts and human will
    Are lost in heavenly glory.

HYMN

AMONG THE ALPS.

No. 1.

O Lord, on this Thy holy day
I upward wend my weary way,
My soul aspiring as I climb,
Mid snowy alpine heights sublime,
That these high steps may be to me
Like stairways leading, Lord, to Thee.

As high the slippery paths I tread,
Be high the thoughts that fill my head;
May they be like Thy glaciers pure,
And like the eternal rocks endure!
Thou only art my hope and stay,
Oh guide and guard me on my way.

AMONG THE ALPS.

No. II.

ROM this great Alp I gaze, and see
No living thing to gladden me,
Like yonder peak, or this lone tree,
O Lord, I feel alone with Thee!

Alone with Thee in word and thought,
In close and sweet communion brought.
Though sin my life has sadly marred,
Like rocky mountains torrent scarred.

Without Thee, loneliness were death,
I feel Thee in the glacier's breath,
I see Thy throne amid the snow,
And hear Thee in the stream below.

Some distant chimes so clear and sweet
Direct me where Thy people meet.
I hate their form, yet join the prayer,
And trust, O Lord, to meet Thee there.

AT LAUSANNE.

HARK! the evening bells are ringing
    O'er the lake, so sweet and clear,
Hark the chorus!—peasants sing-
    ing—
    Distant now—now seeming near:
"Loudly sing, as daylight closes,
Sweet the rest that night imposes."

Stars begin to glimmer faintly,
    Deeper, darker grows the even;
Pilgrims wending, slow and saintly,
    Lift their voice of praise to Heaven,
"Men may hate us, scorn, neglect us!
In our wandering, Lord, protect us!"

O'er the hills the morn is breaking,
    Fringing all the clouds with gold—
Myriad singing-birds awaking,
    Showering song o'er wood and wold.
Night by night repeats the story,
Day by day reveals the glory!

1865.

PRAYER.

TORMENTED mortal, dry thy tears,
   Heed not the wound that stings
      thy clay,
   Hope sweetly smiles, when faith
      appears
And passion conquered kneels to pray.
Attendant angels listening wait,
   To bear the trembling prayer on high;
Its whispers leap the azure gate,
   And rapture rings along the sky!

By prayer the trackless sea of thought
   A glittering golden path is made,
Through which the wandering spirit's brought
   To Christ, of light the living Head:
There hosts redeemed in glory shine,
   And pealing Hallelujahs raise
To HIM the SAVIOUR all Divine,
   And prayer is drowned in songs of praise.

DR. HAMILTON'S " EXCELSIOR," 1856.

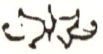

THE DAUGHTER OF JAIRUS.

SUGGESTED BY A PASSAGE IN DR. FARRAR'S "LIFE OF CHRIST."

TALITHA! Talitha! young beautiful maiden!
  Talitha! Talitha! arouse thee, awake!
  Awake, and bring joy to these hearts sorrow laden,
Kind friends all so loving,—so sad for thy sake.

Talitha! Talitha! maiden most beautiful,
  Maiden! Talitha! I bid thee arise!
Arise unresistingly, yieldingly, dutiful;
  Beautiful, dutiful, open thine eyes!

Hushed were all voices: the silence oppressive
  Hung like a curtain in blackness and gloom,
Hoping, yet doubting, alternate, excessive,
  Prevailed in this terrible calm of the tomb;

"Too late! ah, too late! to the voice of the Teacher
  The heart is stone-stiffened; clay closed are the ears!

No voice, howe'er potent, no wise word can reach
 her,
　No power can reopen her fountain of tears!"

ONE form, and ONE only, yields not to the
 grieving,
　Now openly uttered in sobbings and sighs!
HE knew her pale palms from his own were re-
 ceiving
The pulsings which soon would awaken surprise!

Why start they? why gaze they? transfixed in
 their wonder!
　Talitha awakens! she smiles as of yore!
The black seal of death has been broken asunder.
　Talitha has risen!—believers adore.

　1877.

MARTYRDOM.

WHY died the Lord upon the cross?
    Why was He hanged upon the
        tree?
Most strange that darkness, death,
        and loss
    Should light, and life, and blessing be.

He died not as the martyr dies,
    In test of zeal and proof of faith;
But as a bleeding sacrifice,
    To conquer sin by sinless death.

The nails! the thorns! the piercing spear,
    Evoked no hopeless, helpless cry!
Triumphant over grief and fear,
    He taught us how to dare and die.

To dare for Truth the tyrant's yoke,
    For Liberty the rack and chain:
Those who would dwarf the soul, provoke
    The vengeance of a Saviour slain.

MARTYRDOM.

To barter Truth for ease or wealth,
    To live on earth a living lie!—
For mental life and spirit health—
    Than living thus, 'twere life to die

No weapons have the power to kill
    The martyrs suffering for the Truth:
Their souls released surround us still,
    And flourish in immortal youth.

For God! for Christ they bear the shame—
    The scoff—the taunt—the biting rod!
Proud to be worthy of the name
    Of martyrs suffering for their God.

Thus dying, they to all bequeathed
    A heritage which all should give,
Untainted, pure and freely breathed!
    They perished that the Truth might live.

From seed thus sown in faith and love
    Spring harvests of the living bread;
The world was lost with Christ alive,
    Now all is Life by Jesus dead!

THE WAYSIDE CROSS

AMONG THE VOSGES MOUNTAINS.

THAT wayside cross upon the hill,
How desolate when winds blow chill,
And clouds their icy tears distil!

A simple cross so high and lone,
Of rudest form and roughest stone,
Where plaintive winds perpetual moan.

And moaning there rise many a sigh
From heavy hearts—the weeping eye
Unheeded by the passer by!

Here wasted forms with matted hair;
Victims of passion, in despair
Would shuffle off their robe of care.

A robe wrought in the living loom,
Where every flower of life might bloom,
Now shrouded by the clouds of doom.

The lorn, the lost, in rage and pain
For succour fly to it, and rain
Their burning tears to cool the brain!

Soul-sick and weary, sad and weak,
With tottering gait and channelled cheek:
God grant the comfort that they seek!

And will they find it? Who can tell—
Whilst love supreme and mercy dwell
Where hearts with thoughts repentant swell?

Oh, will they find it? Who dare say
That HE the Just will mercy stay,
When thus forlorn, His children pray?

Though fierce corroding sin oppressed,
The shelter gained, the sin confessed,
The sinner may be shrived and blessed.

It may be folly, but it steals
Like balm into their heart, and heals
When conscience roused, its stain reveals.

"The creed is false!"—it may be true,
But true or false, if it subdue
The wrong in them, 'tis right and true.

Lo! here the profligate and vile,
Depraved and outcast, for a while
May find a home, and learn to smile!

The reckless outlaw's last resource,
Victim and villain—with remorse,—
May faint and falter in his course!

And here the weeping Magdalene,
Upon the mountain top unseen,
May clasp the cross and rise serene!

In every scene of gain or loss,
In this great world of pitch and toss,
'Tis well for men to mark the cross.

With holy zeal, where crosses stand
In town, on tower, or mountain land,
Their spirit makes the heart expand.

Blest emblems of a faith divine,
Like beacons on a hill they shine!
Accept the truth, adopt the sign!

They point to heaven, the spirit's goal,
They cheer the heart, exalt the soul,
And make the wounded spirit whole.

Methinks I see an angel there,
Listening, with outspread wings to bear
On high the penitential prayer.

All glory be to God, since they
So late cast down, rise bright and gay,
And pass rejoicing on their way!

The curtain of the clouds is riven,
The cross is smit with rays from heaven,—
Our God in light has answer given!

NOTES.

NOTES.

Introductory Note from the History of the Fairfax Family.

SOME two years after the publication of SIR RALPH DE RAYNE and LILIAN GREY, my friend Miss Oakley, who had been reading the life of the great LORD FAIRFAX, drew my attention to a passage in the work, which I here append, showing, as it does, how nearly a work, purely imaginative, may approach circumstances and events which have absolutely occurred, and are historically vouched for.—F. B.

"A noteworthy story attached to the marriage of the second SIR WILLIAM FAIRFAX. In the lowland, some four miles away from Steeton, near the junction of the rivers Ouse and Wharfe, stood the very small but ancient Cistercian Nunnery of Appleton, which was presided over by the last abbess, the Lady ANNA LANGTON. A young lady named Isabella Thwaites, who was an orphan, and a great heiress, had been placed under the guardianship of Nunappleton Abbess.

She had been allowed to visit friends in the neighbourhood, and she and young William Fairfax loved each other. But the scheming abbess had other views for her young ward. She forbade the Fairfax lover to approach the nunnery, and confined her ward within its walls. At last an order was obtained from higher authorities to release the girl. But even then it was found necessary to make a forcible entry into the nunnery; and Isabel was carried off in triumph, to be married to young Fairfax at BOLTON ABBEY.

"This was a most fortunate and auspicious union, and from it descended all the statesmen and warriors, scholars and poets, who rendered famous the ancient house of Fairfax. Long afterwards, when the family was less prosperous, there was an old Yorkshire saying:—

> "'Fairfax shall regain
> The glory that has fled,
> When Steeton once again
> Nunappleton shall wed.'

"Isabel Thwaites brought to her husband the estates of Denton and Ashworth, in beautiful Wharfedale, and those of Bishop Hill and Davy Hall, within the walls of York.

"Sir William Fairfax, of Steeton, lived for many years with his beautiful Isabel, and was a very influential knight in Yorkshire. He joined the Pilgrimage of Grace; yet, long afterwards. Henry VIII. addressed him as 'his trusty and well-beloved knight.' It was a remarkable retribution that Nunappleton, where fair Isabel had been so ill used by the abbess, should, at the Reformation, have been granted to the Fairfaxes on

December 5th, 1542. The same hard, unfeeling ANNA LANGTON had to surrender her nunnery to Thomas and Guy, the young sons of Sir William and Isabel, who pulled down the religions buildings and erected a house out of part of the materials. An old stone with 'Guido Fairfax' carved upon it, now forms part of the bridge over the stream that flows into the Wharfe at Nunappleton."

Note 1. Page 26.

Sir Ralph de Rayne and Lilian Grey.

(Page 25.)

[The Author thanks Mrs. Nicholson, widow of Dr. Nicholson, so long the beloved Rector of the Abbey Church, for many useful hints, and would express his obligations to the friends who supplied other information.]

The Society of Noviomagus was founded in consequence of a small party of Fellows of the Society of Antiquaries having agreed to make an excavation at Holwood, near Keston, in Kent, on the spot which was supposed by Stillingfleet and other antiquaries to be the Roman station of Noviomagus, mentioned in the Itinerary of Antoninus.

About a quarter of a mile from the Roman works called "Cæsar's Camp" is a tumulus, known even at the present day as the "War bank," and here the party commenced operations. They discovered the foundations of a temple and several ancient stone coffins, Roman remains, &c.

These were described in a paper read before the Society of Antiquaries on the 27th November, 1828, by Mr. Alfred J. Kempe, followed by another paper by T. Crofton Croker. Mr. Balmanno and Mr. W. H. Brooke were also present.

After a meeting of the Society of Antiquaries on the 11th December, 1828, a small party interested in the matter adjourned to Cork Street, Burlington Gardens, and a society, " to be called the Society of Noviomagus," was then and there instituted. The following week, the same party being present, these were elected :—

T. Crofton Croker	President.
A. J. Kempe	Vice-President.
Robert Lemon	Treasurer.
H. Brandreth	Poet Laureate.
W. H. Brooke	Principal Artist in Ordinary.
Robert Balmanno	Secretary, *pro tem.*
John Rouse	Usher of the Black Rod.

Subsequently the following gentlemen were elected :—

W. Jerdan	Father Confessor.
W. H. Rosser	Secretary.
J. Bowyer Nicholls	Typographer.
Rev. J. Lindsay	Chamberlain.
Sir William Betham	Genealogist.
J. R. Planche	Dramatist.
Thomas Saunders	Attorney-General.
W. J. Thoms, F.S.A.	Notes and Queries.
William Wansey, F.S.A.	The Fishmonger.
F. W. Fairholt, F.S.A.	The Draughtsman.

They met every Thursday evening, after leaving Somerset House, at some convenient place in the neighbourhood, to partake of a supper, which, in those primitive days, consisted of Welsh rarebits, potatoes and butter. Glenlivat whisky, lemons, and sugar: and, at the close of the session, a trip was arranged to Keston Cross or some other place of interest.

The members at the time the LEGEND was published were :—

The Lord High President	S. C. Hall, F.S.A.
The Baronet	Sir F. G. Moon, Bt., F.S.A.
The Architect. . . .	George Godwin, F.S.A.
The Physician . . .	Dr. Stevenson, F.S.A.
The American Minister	Henry Stevens, F.S.A.
The Sculptor	Joseph Durham, F.S.A.
The ex-Sheriff . . .	Charles Hill, F.S.A.
The Librarian . . .	Joshua W. Butterworth, F.S.A.
The Photographer . .	Dr. Hugh Diamond, F.S.A.
The Friar	Edwin H. Lawrence, F.S.A.
The Absentee . . .	Charles Ratcliffe, F.S.A.
The Associate . . .	Wm. Chaffers (late), F.S.A.
Treasurer, Laureate, & Acting Secretary .	Francis Bennoch, F.S.A.

Thirteen being the original number of members enrolled, continues a rule of the brotherhood.

The list of members remains the same this year (1877), with the exception of The BARONET—deceased: and the ASSOCIATE—retired. But, with the addition of—

The Merchant . . .	Charles J. Leaf, F.S.A.
The State Physician	Dr. Richardson, F.S.A.
The Public Orator .	Wyke Bayliss, F.S.A.
The Book Worm .	George Bullen, F.S.A.

The number is therefore now fifteen, which is in perfect accordance with the understanding that a law broken, is *the* law observed!

Note 2. Page 27.

"*Martyr Alban's Town,*" also "*Abbey Church.*"
(Pages 27 and 28.)

In respect of situation there are few abbeys in England superior to that of St. Albans, standing as it does, so grandly on the side of a hill, surrounded by a large extent of richly varied and interesting landscape. On the other side of the Ver are the gentle slopes of ancient Verulam, and beyond and around are lovely heights covered with noble woods, producing effects of beauty and richness of effect probably unequalled. An old rhyme says:—

> "When Verulam stood,
> St. Albans was a wood;
> Now Verulam's down,
> St. Albans is a town."

Note 3. Pages 27 and 28.

St. Albans and Verulam.

The finest view of St. Albans is obtained from the south side, on the raised ground, where still, in the ruins of the massy walls, may be traced the power of the Romans, the once mighty conquerors of the world, and the extent of the ancient and great city of Verulam, from which St. Alban went forth to the grassy slopes of the opposite hill, resolved and willing to die as the first British martyr to the faith in Christ. From this eminence, the site of ancient Verulam, the view is one of picturesque beauty. Where St.

Alban shed his blood, rises in majestic grandeur the venerable Abbey Church, surrounded, or nearly so, by the modern town of St. Albans. The little river Ver, from which the ancient city took its name, meanders gracefully through the valley, until it joins the Colne, some four miles to the south-east. In the summer time, the fertile fields of waving corn, the green meadows, and the sylvan scenery, complete a picture which the mind cannot contemplate without pleasurable emotion.—MASON.

The Holy Alban was slain because he had sheltered, and allowed to escape, Amphibolous, a deacon of the Christian Church, and brought upon himself the death from which he had rescued his friend. Many churches were built, and dedicated to the name of the proto-martyr, notably St. Alban's, Wood Street, which was built by Offa, King of the Mercians, and used as his chapel, being contiguous to his palace in London.

Note 4.

Lilian Grey. (Page 28.)

Edmond, Earl of Kent, was originally Lord Grey of Ruthyn, and created Earl by Edward IV. He had a son, Sir Anthony Grey, whose mother was daughter of Henry Percy, Earl of Northumberland. It has been stated that he was killed at the battle of St. Albans; this, however, is doubted: some confusion having arisen between Grey of Ruthyn and Sir John Grey of Groby, killed in the battle, fighting on the side of Lancaster; and his widow, Elizabeth Woodville, became the Queen of Edward IV.—Dr. Nicholson.

The precise relationship of Lilian Grey to these noble houses, it is difficult now to determine.

Note 5.

Gorhambury and St. Michael. (Page 28.)

On the floor is the brass effigy of Rauff (Ralph) Rowlott, merchant of the Staple at Calais, an ancient company of foreign merchants, incorporated by Edward III. He was the lineal ancestor of Sarah, Duchess of Marlborough. The estates of Gorhambury and Sandridge, with others, had been granted to him by Henry VIII. at the dissolution of the monastery. His son dying, his two daughters became co-heiresses. Mary or Margery, the eldest, inherited Gorhambury, and married John Maynard, Esq., of Easting, in the county of Essex, who sold the whole of his estate in the neighbourhood of St. Albans to Sir Nicholas Bacon, Knight, afterwards Lord Keeper of the Great Seal in the reign of Queen Elizabeth. Bacon was buried in St. Michael's Church.

The ancient Watling Street seems to have passed a little to the southward of St. Michael's Church, and led past Gorhambury, the residence of the Earl of Verulam, where a portion of the ruins of the mansion of Robert de Gorham, and where Lord Bacon resided, may still be seen.—Dr. Nicholson.

Note 6.

"*From Sopwell's cloisters.*" (Page 28.)

Matthew Paris relates that two women having entered on a recluse life in a hut which they had constructed near the river, the abbot built a house for their better accommodation, placing therein thirteen sisters under the rule of St. Benedict. As the first two women used to dip their dry bread in the water of a neighbouring spring, the place was called Sopwell, or *Sop in the Well.*

Books were printed at St. Albans as early as the year 1480. The first treatise on hunting which ever issued from the press was the " Boke of Saint Alban," written by Dame Juliana Barns (otherwise Berners), the Prioress of Sopwell, and printed in the monastery, 1486, a copy of which is in the collection of Earl Spencer, and another in the University Library, Cambridge. It is divided into three sections: one on hunting, one on fishing, and one on coat armour—a curious study for a nun.—DR. NICHOLSON's *History.*

Note 7.

"*Should seek the Abbey Church.*" (Page 28.)

In 1077, Paul, of the Abbey of Caen, in Normandy, was appointed to preside over St. Albans, and within eleven years constructed the greater part of the Abbey Church. He was powerfully assisted by his kinsman Lanfranc, Archbishop of Canterbury, who was succeeded by Anselm, Abbot of Bec. The new church was magnificently dedicated on the 5th of the Kalends of January, 1115, by Geoffrey, Archbishop of Rouen, assisted by Robert, Bishop of Lincoln, Roger of Sarum, Ralph of Durham, and Richard of London, and many more abbots, in the presence of King Henry I., Matilda his Queen, and many earls, barons, nobles—illustrious personages of whom the number is unknown because of the multitude; on which day all remained feasting and rejoicing in the Court of St. Alban, the blessed Protomartyr of the English.—BUCKLER's *History*, p. 5, &c.

Note 8.

"*Miller's lake-like dam.*"   (Page 32.)

"Many buildings in the occupation of the Abbey stood in its immediate vicinity: the Grange and the Mill were ranged towards the west, and extended over a considerable surface, and large tracts of land, including the orchards, pasturage, and fishpools stretched along the southern side, supplying by their various stores the constant demands of hospitality, contributing in no small degree to the character and splendour of the domain."—BUCKLER's *History*, p. 166.

Note 9.

"*Old heathen Verulam, whose stones.*"   (Page 32.)

Matthew Paris expressly records the fact that the ruins of Verulam were resorted to for supplying materials for the re-edification of the church.

The evidence seems irresistible that the material was not made for the Church of St. Albans, but that the building was to some extent designed to suit the materials. The bricks and tiles were doubtless formed eight centuries before the time when they were used to construct a Christian church, and may have been taken from the theatre or the temple of the gods. From the foundation to the uppermost courses of the walls, even to the parapet of the tower, is of tile construction. Verulam, with the addition of some portions of the old Saxon church, which was wholly destroyed, served to construct the new building of the Abbey Church.

The bricks were very large, measuring $16 \times 12 \times 1\frac{1}{2}$; and one discovered on the site of Verulam, and preserved at Oaklands, weighs 21 lbs.—*Condensed from* BUCKLER's *History*, p. 22, &c.

Note 10.

"*The stately column.*" (Page 33.)

The most remarkable instance of attempting to harmonize the different periods of architecture occurs in the eighth pillar from the west end on the north side of the nave. The broad members in the front, and in one reveal, have been formed with segments of circles, and the intermediate angles sloped off—a rude resemblance of the clustered columns opposite, and at the west end—but the attempt was not sufficiently encouraging to be persisted in, and the mutilated column remains, as it was left, unfinished by the workmen.—BUCKLER's *History*, p. 144.

Note 11.

"*The stately column's clustered stone.*" (Page 33.)

Here we observe the Norman or Romanesque style of the twelfth century, the Early English or first Gothic style of the thirteenth century, and the Decorated style of the fourteenth century. The place on the north series of arches, where the Norman ends and the Gothic begins, deserves notice. The clustered Early English pillars of the sixth arch of the nave spring *out of* the massive Norman pier.—MASON.

Note 12.

"*And pierced the neck of Ralph de Rayne.*" (Page 35.)

The first battle of St. Albans was fought on the 23rd May, 1455, between Henry VI. and Richard, Duke of York. A strong party, led by the Earl of Warwick, burst into the town with great shouting, and overcame the royal army, which lost heart and fled. The king, finding himself alone, and deserted, *and wounded in the neck by an arrow,* took refuge in a small cottage occupied by a baker, where he was found by the Duke of York, who with all courtesy conducted the crestfallen monarch first to the Abbey, and next day to London.—MASON.

Note 13.

"*The Priest in grand array of state.*" (Page 38.)

In the British Museum there is a picture headed " The Parliament holden at Westminster the fourth of Feb., the third yeare of our Sovereigne Lord King Henry the 8th, A.D. 1572," during the rule of Abbot Ramayge, in which the figure and dress of each ecclesiastic dignitary are depicted: abbots of least note lead the procession two and two first, and then those of higher dignity, the Abbot of Tewkesbury and the Prior of Coventry leading, and the Abbots of St. Albans and Westminster are the last pair.

All the abbots, with two exceptions, have the same dress—a plain cassock and cap with an ample robe of purple, having folds behind as a hood. None of the abbots wear mitres. The bishops wear the same simple caps as the abbots, and only the archbishops, who close the procession, wear the mitre.—NICHOLSON.

Robert de Gorham was the first abbot on whom the mitre was conferred, and the Abbots of St. Albans were authorized by the Pope to take precedence of all others in England.—MASON's Guide.

Note 14.

"*Where great Duke Humphrey lies in state.*"

(Page 38.)

Humphrey, Duke of Gloucester, who died at Bury, February 28th, 1447, was buried in the Church of St. Albans, where a superb monument was erected to his memory. He was fourth and youngest son of Henry IV., and Protector of the Kingdom during the minority of his nephew, Henry VI.

The iron grating is generally considered to be

of a date prior to the erection of the monument, and was intended to give to pilgrims, and other visitors in the aisle, a view of the shrine in the centre of the Feretory, or Saint's Chapel.

Duke Humphrey founded the Divinity School at Oxford, and commenced the collection of books which formed the nucleus of the Bodleian Library; though all, save two, of the books presented by him were destroyed by the Visitors in the time of Edward VI.

The story of his death—murder rather—at Bury St. Edmunds, and the details of the removal of his body to St. Albans, were published by the Camden Society in 1856.

Note 15.

"*His left hand held a feathery palm.*" (Page 39.)

On the 5th December, 1539, the king's commissioners came to St. Albans, when the fortieth abbot, Richard Boreman, *alias* De Stevenache, signed a deed of surrender, and delivered up the seal of the monastery, which is now in the British Museum. It is made of ivory, and represents St. Alban holding in his hand a branch of the palm-tree.—MASON.

Note 16.

Shrine. (Page 39.)

Abbot Geoffrey, in the fifth year of his prelacy, commenced a glorious shrine of marvellous workmanship for the Blessed Alban, our patron. . . . . And he made it of hammered work raised and brought out, and he filled in the hollows with cement, and completed the elegance of the whole body of the shrine by a steeply raised ridge, and this still further beautified the whole.

And when all the parts of the shrine were thus handsomely executed, he had the whole richly gilt, so that they rather appeared to be of gold than silver. From the ancient treasury of the church jewels were brought forth for its decoration—one sardonyx being of such size that it could scarcely be held in one hand, and none other was like unto it. This unrivalled stone was given to the church by King Etheldred, the father of Edward, the most pious king of England. All being prepared, the remains of the Holy Alban were duly translated thereunto on the anniversary of the festival of St. Peter.—*Condensed from* BUCKLER's *History*, p. 48, &c.

Note 17.

"*Till glancing on the Holy Rood.*" (Page 39.)

In the time of Abbot William of Trumpington, Master Walter de Colchester, then Sacrist, an incomparable painter and sculptor, erected a loft or *pulpitum* in the middle of the church, with its great Rood and Mary and John, and other carvings and handsome decorations, at the cost of the Sacristy, but by the diligence of his own labour.

The altar was solemnly dedicated by John, Bishop of Ardfert, in honour of the Holy Cross, and the same bishop consecrated the great Rood, which, with its images, was placed over this altar. From which it is evident that an altar in honour of the Holy Cross, enclosed by an iron screen, stood at the entrance to the Sanctuary.—BUCKLER's *History*, p. 70.

Note 18.

" *From fretted roof and cloisters dim.*" (Page 41.)

Abbot Robert, in the twelfth century, erected one cloister along the east side. Abbot Trumpington constructed several others, chiefly of oak timber, some of which remain. Abbot Roger, who so greatly adorned the interior of the church, built a cloister against the south wall of the nave, in a superb style of architecture. The unrivalled elegance of the design baffles any attempt at description, and the hand which performed the work with such extraordinary delicacy and beauty had attained its utmost skill. But nothing now remains of this work than that which could not easily be severed from the wall of the church.— *Condensed from* BUCKLER's *History*, p. 258.

Note 19.

" *The veil and wreath,*" &c. (Page 42.)

In the south aisle of the nave hangs the framework of a chaplet, and the tradition has been handed down, that it formed a part of a marriage garland of a bride, who died on her wedding-day, and was said to have been buried near the spot. —MASON.

[If considerable liberty has been taken with dates, the unities of the poem may plead an excuse; and I learn, with pleasure, that a niece of Dr. Nicholson has supplied the new wreaths for many years past.]

Note 20.

" *Ring the bells.*" (Page 42.)

The Abbot Paul furnished the tower with bells, and a certain noble named Litholf, who resided in a woodland part of the neighbourhood, added one still larger and more laudable than the rest. Having a good stock of sheep and goats, he sold many of them and bought a bell, of which, as he heard the new sound when suspended in the tower, he said jocosely, " Hark! how sweetly my goats and my sheep bleat." His wife procured another bell for the same place, and the two together produced the most sweet harmony, which, when the lady heard, she said: " I do not think this union is wanting of the Divine favour, which united me to my husband in lawful matrimony and the bond of mutual affection."—BUCKLER'S *History.*

Note 21.

" *The Organ swells.*" (Page 43.)

John of Wheathampstead was re-elected Abbot in 1451, and about this time gave to his church a pair of organs, on which and their erection he spent fifty pounds.

No organ in any monastery in England was comparable to one of these for size, and tone, and workmanship.—DR. NICHOLSON.

GLOSSARY.

GLOSSARY.

', all.
Aboon, above.
Ae, one.
Aff, off.
Afore, before.
Aft, oft.
Aften, often.
Aiblins, perhaps.
Ain, own.
Hake, alas.
Alane, alone.
Amaist, almost.
Amang, among.
An', and, if.
Ance, once.
Ane, one.
Anent, over, against.
Anither, another.
Aught, anything, aught.
Auld, old.
Ava, at, all.
Awa, away.
Aufu', awful.
Ayont, beyond.

Ba', ball.
Bairn, child.
Baith, both.
Ban, to swear.
Bane, bone.
Bauld, bold.
Bawsent, white stripe on horse's face.

Ben, parlour.
Benk, book.
Big, to build.
Biggot, built.
Birk, birch.
Birkie, clever lad.
Blate, bashful.
Blaw, to blow.
Bleezing, blazing.
Blether, nonsense.
Bleth'rin, talking idly.
Blink, a little while, a bright smile.
Bluid, blood.
Blithe, cheerful.
Bonnie, or bonny, beautiful.
Bracken, fern.
Brae, the slope of a hill.
Braid, broad.
Brak, broke.
Braw, fine, well clothed.
Breckans, ferns.
Breeks, breeches.
Brent, smooth.
Brig, bridge.
Brither, brother.
Brose, oatmeal and butter, with hot water.
Burn, a small river.
Burnie, a rivulet.
Bushie, bushy.
Buskit, dressed.
But the house, kitchen.
Byre, cow-house.

GLOSSARY.

CA, call.
Ca't, or ca'd, called.
Cadger, carrier.
Cairn, a heap of loose stones.
Callan, boy.
Canie, or cannie, gentle, mild, clever.
Cantie, or canty, cheerful, merry.
Carl, old man.
Carlin, old woman.
Cauld, cold.
Chaft, cheek.
Claes, clothes.
Claivers, nonsense.
Clatter, idle talk.
Clavers, random speech.
Claw, scratch.
Cleckit, hooked, arm-in-arm.
Clinkin', jerking, clinking.
Coila, kyle — Ayrshire dialect.
Collie, shepherd's dog.
Coof, cuif, blockhead, ninny.
Cosie, snug.
Cosily, snugly.
Cotter, cottager.
Coup, or cowp, barter, tumble.
Cowpet, exchanged, tumbled.
Crabbit, fretful.
Craw, crow.
Creel, basket.
Croon, to hum a tune.
Curling, a game on ice.
Cushat, wood pigeon.
Cutty, short.

DADDIE, father.
Daffin, joking, teasing.
Daft, giddy, foolish.

Dainty, nice, agreeable.
Dales, plains, valleys.
Daur, dare.
Deil, devil.
Dight, wipe.
Ding, push.
Dinna, do not.
Dirl, a tremulous sound.
Doited, stupefied.
Douce, clever, prudent.
Doure, sullen.
Dowie, wearied.
Drap, drop.
Dreigh, long, tedious.
Drift, heap of snow.

E'E, eye.
E'en, eyes.
Eerie, spirit frightened.
En', end.
Eneugh, enough.
Ettle, attempted, hoped.
Eydent, diligent.

FA', fall.
Fa's, falling.
Fae, foe.
Faem, foam.
Fand, did find.
Fash, trouble.
Fashed, troubled.
Fauld, a fold, to fold.
Faulding, folding.
Fearfu', fearful.
Fear't, frighted.
Fecht, to fight.
Feck, many, plenty.
Fidge, to fidget.
Fidgen, restless.
Fit, a foot.
Fleech, to supplicate flatteringly.
Fleeched, supplicated.
Fleechen, supplicating.
Fley, to frighten.

GLOSSARY.

Flunkie, servant (male).
Forbye, besides.
Forgather, to meet accidentally.
Forgie, forgive.
Fou, full, intoxicated.
Frae, from.
Frien', friend.
Fu', full.
Fyke, troubled by trifles.

GAB, the mouth.
Gae, go; *gaed*, went; *gaen*, gone; *gaun*, going.
Gait, way, manner, road.
Gang, to go, walk.
Gar, to make, force to.
Gar't, compelled.
Geck, to toss the head.
Ghaist, ghost.
Gie, to give; *gied*, gave; *gien*, given.
Glaikit, foolish.
Gleg, sharp.
Glint, gleam, instant peep.
Glinted, briefly illumined.
Glintin, brief sparkle.
Glower, to stare.
Gowan, daisy, La Marguerite.
Gowany, daisied.
Gowd, gold.
Gowk, cuckoo, simpleton.
Grannie, grandmother.
Grat, wept.
Gree, to agree, conquer.
Greet, to shed tears.
Grun, the ground.
Gude, the Supreme Being.
Guid, good.
Guidman and *guidwife*, master and mistress.
Gully, a large clasp knife.
Gyte, foolish.

HA', hall.
Hae, to have.
Haffets, temples, side of head.
Haivers, nonsense.
Hame, home.
Hamely, homely.
Han, or *haun*, hand.
Hap, to cover.
Haud, to hold.
Haverel, half witted.
Hech, oh, strange.
Herd, to tend flocks.
Het, hot.
Heugh, pit or furrow.
Hirple, to walk lamely.
Hizzie, young woman.
Hog-score, a line across ice rink.
Houlet, owl.
Hurdies, the loins, hips.

I', in.
Ilk, *ilka*, each, every.
Ingle, fire.
Ither, other.

JAD, jade.
Jouk, dally.
Jimp, slender.
Jimpie, very slender.
Jouk, stoop.

KAIL, broth, colewort.
Keek, peep.
Ken, know.
Kenn'd, or *kent*, knew.
Kennen, knowing.
Kennin, a small matter.
Kilt, to truss up petticoats.
Kin', kindred, kind.
Kirn', churn, harvest-feast.
Kith, related.

GLOSSARY.

Kittle, tickle, ticklish.
Knowe, a round hillock.
Kye, cows.
Kyte, belly.

LAD, a youth.
Laddie, small boy.
Laigh, low.
Laith, loath.
Laithfu, bashful.
Lane, lone.
Lanely, lonely.
Lang, long.
Lave, the rest.
Laverock, lark.
Leugh, laughed.
Lift, sky.
Lilt, to sing.
Limmer, wanton woman.
Link, to trip lightly.
Linkin; tripping.
Linn, gorge, waterfall.
Loof, palm of hand.
Loot, did, let.
Loup, jump.
Lug, ear.
Lum, chimney.
Luntin, smoking.
Lyart, mixture with grey.

MAE', more.
Maigrums, notions.
Mair, more.
Maist, most, almost.
Maistly, mostly.
Mak, make.
Mang, among.
Mannikin, endearing term for boy.
Manse, minister's house.
Maun, must.
Mavis, thrush.
Maw, mow.
Mawing, mowing.
Men', to mend.

Mense, good mannerly.
Minnie, mother.
Mirk, mirkest, dark, darkest.
Mither, mother.
Mou', mouth.
Mony, or *monie*, many.
Moorlan', stretch of moors.
Morn, to-morrow.
Muckle, mickle, much.
Mysel, myself.

NA', no, not, nor.
Nae, no, not, nay.
Naething, nothing.
Nappy, ale, liquor.
Neibour, neighbour.
Neuk, corner.
Niest, next.
Nieve, fist.
Nit, nut.
Nowte, black cattle.

O', of.
Och'on, alas.
Ony, any.
O't, of it.
Oursel, oursels, ourself, ourselves.
Owre, over.

PAITRICK, partridge.
Pawky, pawkie, cunning, sly.
Pit, to put.
Pluck, small Scottish coin.
Pluckless, penniless.
Prie, to taste.
Pried, tasted.
Preen, pin.

RASH, rush.
Rattan, rat.
Raw, a row.
Reek, smoke.

Reekin, smoking.
Reekit, smoked.
Rig, a ridge.
Rin, to run, to meet.
Rink, a course on ice.
Rinnin, running.
Roose, to praise.
Roun', round.
Roup, auction.
Roupet, hoarse, sold.
Routh, routhie, very much.
Rung, cudgel, ladder-step.
Runt, cabbage stem.

SAE, so.
Saft, soft.
Sair, sore, to serve.
Sairly, or *sairlie*, sorely.
Sark, shirt.
Saul, soul.
Saut, salt.
Sawin, sowing.
Scaur, precipice, scarred.
Sel, self.
Sen, to send.
Sheen, bright, shining.
Sheugh, ditch.
Shiel, shielin, shelter, shed.
Shoon, shoes.
Shouther, shoulder.
Sic, such.
Sicker, sure, safe.
Siller, silver, money.
Simmer, summer.
Sin, son.
Sin', sin syne, since, ever since.
Skaith, as skath.
Skirl, shriek, shrilly.
Skelp, slap.
Slae, sloe.
Smoor, smoored, smother, smothered.
Snaw, snow.

Sneck, latch.
Snell, keen, cold, bitter.
Snod, neat.
Sonsie, pleasant-looking.
Souter, shoemaker.
Speel, climb.
Spiel, bon spiel, a game, a match.
Spier, to ask.
Spier'd, inquired.
Spunk, fire.
Spunkie, mettlesome, spirited.
Stalwart, tall and strong.
Stan', to stand.
Stane, a stone.
Steek, to shut.
Stey, steep.
Stirk, a young beast.
Stockin', stocking.
Stot, an ox.
Stoup, or *stowp*, a jug or mug.
Stour, dust in motion.
Sugh, low moaning wind.
Swither, to waver in choice.

TAE, gang tae, toe, go to.
Ta'en, taken.
Tane or tither, one or other.
Tap, top.
Tawse, instrument of torture: leather strap split into thongs, used by schoolmasters.
Ted, tedding, to spread, spreading.
Tent, tak tent, care, take care.
Tentie, heedful.
Tentless, heedless.
Thae, these.
Thankit, thanked.
Theekit, thatched.

Thegither, together.
Themsel', themselves.
Thole, to endure.
Thrang, throng.
Thraw, to sprain, twist.
Threshin', thrashing.
Thud, sudden blow or noise.
Thwack, strike.
Thysel, thyself.
Till't, to it.
Tine, tint, to lose, lost.
Tirl, slight vibratory noise.
Tirlin, uncovering.
Tither, the other.
Tocher, marriage portion.
Toddlin, uncertain walking.
Toun, hamlet.
Tout, to blow a horn.
Towsie, rough, shaggy.
Trig, neat.
Trow, to believe.
Trowth, truth.
Tryst, place of meeting.
Trysted, appointed.
Twa, two.
Twal, twelve.
Tyke, a dog.

UNCO, strange, very great.
Unkenned, unknown.
Upo', upon.

VAPRIN', vapouring.

WA', *wa's*, wall, walls.
Wad, would.
Wadna, would not.
Wae, woe, sorrow.
Waefu', woful, sorrowful.
Waft, woof, waved.

Wale, to wale, choice, to choose.
Waled, chosen.
Wame, belly.
Wark, work.
Warl, world.
Warst, worst.
Wat, wot, wot, I know.
Waukit, thickened, awakened.
Waur, waurst, worse, worst.
Wean, weanie, child.
Wearie, feeble, tired.
Weasened, shrivelled.
Wee, little.
Weel, well.
Weet, wet, rainy.
Wha, who
Whase, whose.
Whaur, where.
Whiles, sometimes.
Whingin, fretting, complaining.
Whisht be whisht, quiet, silence, be quiet.
Wifie, wifiekin, endearing term for wife, or little wife.
Wimple, to meander with a ripple.
Wimplin, waving.
Win, winnow, wind.
Winna, will not.
Winnock, window.
Winsome, attractive, hearty.
Wird, mad.
Wiss, wish.
Wizened, harsh hided.
Wonner, wonder.
Woo, to court, make love.
Wow, exclamation of surprise.
Wraith, a ghost, spirit.

W'rang, wrong.
W'yle, beguile.
W'yte, blame, fault.

YAUD, a horse.
Ye', often used as *thou*.
Yearns, longs for.
Year is used for plural also.

Yell, barren.
Yestreen, yesternight.
Yett, gate.
Yill, ale.
Yont, beyond.
Yowe, ewe.
Yoursel, yourself.
Yule, Christmas.

THE END.

CHISWICK PRESS:—C. WHITTINGHAM, TOOKS COURT,
CHANCERY LANE.

www.ingramcontent.com/pod-product-compliance
Lightning Source LLC
Chambersburg PA
CBHW032142010526
44111CB00035B/901